Best Tennis Humor

IT ONLY HURTS WHEN I SERVE

Best Tennis Humor

IT ONLY HURTS WHEN I SERVE

Edited by David Wiltse

A
tennis
MAGAZINE
BOOK

ACKNOWLEDGMENTS

"Nobody Beats Mason" by Leonard S. Bernstein from the Kansas Quarterly, Volume 11, Number 3, Summer 1979, copyright © 1979 by Leonard S. Bernstein. Reprinted by permission of the author.

"Teddy Tinling on Tour", "Tennis with Ustinov" and "Sleepwalking with Rod Laver" by Gordon Forbes from "A Handful of Summers", copyright © 1978 by Gordon Forbes. Reprinted by permission of Mayflower Books, Inc.

"House Guest 40, Host 0" by David Wiltse from Tennis Magazine, March 1980, copyright © 1980 by Tennis Magazine. (Original title "We Invited A Tournament Player To Stay . . . and Little Did We Know!")

"On Court with the Beautiful People" by Art Buchwald from Tennis Magazine, September 1973, copyright © 1973 Tennis Magazine. (Original title "Art Buchwald on court with the Kennedys.")

"It's not Love but it's not Bad!" by Richard R. Szathmary from Tennis Magazine, March 1978, copyright © 1978 by Tennis Magazine. (Original title "The Tennis Singles Party: 'It's Not Love, But It's Not Bad' ")

"No. 1—For a Week" by Barry Tarshis from Tennis Magazine, March 1977, copyright © 1977 by Tennis Magazine. (Original title "Instant Stardom: I Went From Hacker to No. 1 Overnight")

"The Racquet as Scalpel" by William Walden from Tennis Magazine, January 1973, copyright © 1973 by Tennis Magazine.

Published by Golf Digest/Tennis, Inc.
A New York Times Company
495 Westport Avenue
Norwalk, Connecticut 06856

Trade book distribution by
Simon & Schuster
A Division of Gulf + Western
    Corporation
New York, New York 10020

First Printing
ISBN: 0-914178-37-7
Library of Congress: 80-66687
Manufactured in the
    United States of America

Book and jacket design by Dorothy Geiser.
Typesetting by J & J Typesetters, Norwalk, CT.
Printing and binding by R. R. Donnelley & Sons.

Contents

CARTOONISTS whose works appear in this book: Frank Baginski, Glenn Bernhardt, Bo Brown, Evan Diamond, Napier Dunn, David Harbaugh, Wayne Kaneshiro, Edwin Lepper, Walt Miller and Doug Redfern.

Foreword

The game of tennis is not funny in itself. You will not hear many tales of the time Buffy Parkington sliced his serve into the clubhouse and the ball ended up in the vicar's tea cup, the way you will of golf. You will not often play on strange courts in exotic lands, guided by an ancient caddie who knew Bobby Burns and can hit a ball three hundred yards with a gnarled briar pipe. You will not be treated to droll recollections of the time in the 1920's when the wily old spitballer from the Ozarks accidentally put glue on his cap instead of slippery elm and got knocked for a ground-rule double. Tennis does not lend itself to many such stories, because it is not a leisurely sport, like golf or baseball, and does not provide long boring stretches in which to dream up anecdotes.

Funny tennis stories do not tend to come from the skilled players. Bjorn Borg is not essentially funny. Brilliant, but not humorous. The skilled players, after all, have pretty well mastered their inner conflicts. They know what they can do and proceed to do it. Tennis humor arises from a different source—the uncoordinated trying to play a very difficult sport with high expectations of success. It is the vast majority of the unskilled who are providing the slapstick out there.

Tennis is a great leveler, the ultimate democratizer of sport. As they used to say of a gun in gangster movies, it is an equalizer. You have to leave all the hard-earned accomplishments of the rest of your life behind you when you step on the court. Your doctorate in physics does you no good in putting topspin on the ball. Being president of your own blue-chip company does you no good—unless you play your employees, of course. Being beautiful may allow you your pick of partners, but it won't give you a decent second serve. When you play tennis, you must put aside all the carefully constructed defenses and disguises and social stratagems which you've spent a lifetime building and start all over.

The problem, of course, is that none of us can truly lay our identities totally aside and start fresh. There may be a true tabula rasa walking around on Har-tru somewhere, his slate squeaky clean and begging for instructional input, but I have yet to meet him. The rest of us walk around with shreds and scraps and tail ends of our real selves sticking out from under our tennis clothes. We are none of us just tennis players, we are people who have come to expect certain things from life and continue to expect them when we play tennis. Things such as a modicum of order, control, respect, proficiency, dignity. The tennis ball offers us none of that.

We don't get what we expect, of course—unless we expect massive humiliation—and it is from this conflict between expectations and reality that humor arises.

In other words, tennis humor is not about others, it is about ourselves. It is only to the extent that we recognize our own foibles and frustrations that we identify and smile.

I began to make a public spectacle of myself in my early thirties. Before that, I had usually confined my lunacies to the privacy of my own home with only my wife present to descry my foolishness. I never much minded that my wife witnessed my making a fool of myself. She, after all, is constrained by law and sacrament to put up with it.

Then my wife got pregnant and I took up tennis. Since that seemingly innocent decision, I have been making a fool of myself in public places with great regularity, cursing, stomping and mis-hitting in full view of the innocent and hardened alike. It's enough to make a man weep. Or laugh. I chose the latter. So did the other writers represented in this collection. I hope you will too.

—*David Wiltse*
Weston, Conn.
August 1980

Nobody Beats Mason

**LEONARD S.
BERNSTEIN**

I have to tell you about the extraordinary tennis match between Tony Mancuso and Mason Delacourt.

Mason is the number one player at our club which is what happens when you learn to play tennis at the age of seven. At seven, in the country clubs of Greenwich, Connecticut, Mason had already developed a backhand. Most of the guys at the club, at the age of thirty-seven, have still not developed a backhand, which is one of the reasons why nobody beats Mason.

Mason is also beautiful on a tennis court. Like an eagle in flight—like a gazelle on the African Plains—Mason seems to the tennis court born. He's six-two or three, lean, and incredibly graceful. He gets way down on his backhand and follows through on his forehand. His volley dies on the spot. His serve skips to the right or left. He is poetry and majesty blended, and just about everything all the rest of us would like to be.

It would be easy to dislike all that talent but nobody dislikes Mason. He plays with everybody, talks to everybody, and tells funny stories about how his father made him learn tennis when nobody had ever heard of tennis and all the guys were playing football and basketball. No wonder my serve skips, he seems to be saying. It makes us feel better, because none of us has a serve that skips, and we all secretly feel that if we had learned tennis at seven instead of twenty-seven we'd all play like Mason.

So Mason is our idol and Mason is our pride. When we bring a guest we point out Mason. When we talk about tennis we talk about Mason. When we sit around on the patio we sit near him and we listen to what he says. Mason always has stories about how Jack Kramer used to come to his club in Greenwich and play against the pro. And he always knows everything about the current players. "The fastest guy on the courts is Tom Okker," he'll say. And someone else will say Nastase. And Mason will say, "Well, maybe today. Maybe Okker's lost a step. But up to a year ago it was Okker."

And we will all nod to each other because that has to be the truth, and we will all feel safe about repeating Mason's stories to anyone.

Mason beats me about 6-2. I've never won a set from him. Once I had him 4-2 and I thought I might win it. It wasn't that I was playing well because even if I play with divine inspiration I still haven't the strokes to beat Mason. But once in a while Mason will string together some errors, and this was one of those rare times. He came out of it though and beat me 6-4. I actually felt terrific about getting four games from him.

After the morning games we sit around on the patio, drink Cokes, and talk about tennis. It's an important part of the day because that's when you can tell everyone that you lost to Mason 6-4. Losing to Mason 6-4 is better than beating anyone else. The object is to let everyone know about it without appearing pompous. Hopefully someone will ask you. If not, you have to force it. It's a cardinal rule that you never force it if you *won*. That would be incredibly bad taste. You just don't go around saying, "I beat Marty 6-1 this morning." But if you've lost it's possible to mention it. You might start off by saying something like, "I guess I'll never beat Mason." Someone might respond, "How did it go?" And you answer, "Well, I got four games." And everyone turns his head because that's the tennis event of the weekend.

Of course you have to be careful how you answer when someone says, "How did it go?" You couldn't just casually say, "Six-four, Mason." That would seem like you consider it a possibility that you can get four games from him. Bragging. Absolutely. Very bad. If anyone gets four games from Mason he had better show appropriate surprise.

A lot of thought goes into the after-tennis conversation. For instance, let's say you got badly beaten by a player who shouldn't beat you at all. You don't go around asking everyone else how they did. The result of asking is that you get asked.

Also, if you've just been beaten, you don't drink your

Coke in the busiest circle on the patio. *Someone* is sure to ask you. Better to walk over and watch one of the matches or maybe check out the seeding on the tournament chart.

On the other hand, if you beat someone who you have no business beating, you naturally squeeze into a crowded spot and stir up an absolute whirlwind of tennis talk.

That's the way it is. I can't help it. Am I responsible for the egos of thirty million tennis players?

Before I tell you about the extraordinary match, I have to tell you about Tony Mancuso. Tony's about five-six, very dark, and very Italian. He has thick tufts of hair on his arms and a handlebar mustache. He usually sits alone and he always seems morose and brooding. We call him—though not to his face because Tony is a very strong guy—the organ grinder.

The organ grinder learned tennis maybe five years ago when he was about thirty. He has terrible strokes or at least they seem terrible, mainly because they are clumsy. Nevertheless, Tony beats most of the guys who have good strokes, and he does this because he is very fast, very determined, very athletic, and somehow manages to get the ball over the net all the time, which, like it or not, is what wins a tennis point.

Nobody sits with Tony on the patio and I think it's because Tony never talks about interesting things like whether Okker is faster than Nastase. I know I don't like to sit with him because, among other things, he might ask me to play a set, and I *definitely* don't want to play a set against the organ grinder because he'll probably beat me on pure determination, and I'll probably have to admit it on the patio.

Mason doesn't think about things like that. Mason plays everybody. If you ask him for a game and if he doesn't have one, he plays you. I don't think he worries a lot about who is good and who is bad. Maybe, if I had a backhand, I wouldn't think about those things either.

One morning I finished a match at about ten o'clock, and on one of the far courts Mason is playing Tony Mancuso. Nice of Mason, I thought. I watch the match for about a minute and although I'm pretty far away I see Mason put a volley into the net, and I see Mancuso walk to the net to shake his hand. Mancuso shake his hand? Impossible. It can only mean one thing; the match is over and Mancuso won. I think about it a while. Probably Mason won. But no, there's no question about it. Whoever wins the last point *must* win the match.

They both walk over to the patio and sit down, but it's only ten o'clock and everyone is still on the courts. Mason wanders off somewhere and Mancuso picks out a seat in the center of a group of seven or eight chairs. I get a Coke and look for someone to sit next to, but the patio is empty except for Mancuso so I have no choice.

"Who did you play this morning?" he asks.

"I played Peter. He beat me in a tiebreaker." I might as well mention the score because he's going to ask me anyway.

Now protocol demands that I return the question. Certainly, *knowing* that Tony just beat Mason, it would be absolutely unforgivable not to return the question. Tony has moved up to the edge of his seat. He's almost smiling.

"Nice day for the beach," I say.

Tony slumps back in the chair but he doesn't give up. "Gee, you should beat Peter. How did it get to a tiebreaker?"

"Well, I had him 5-3. Missed eight backhands in a row. It got up to 6-6 and he won the tiebreaker."

"Did you ever play Mason?" Tony asks relentlessly. He has the conversation back on the track.

"Yeah, I've played him. Sometimes I even get a game or two. Once I caught him when his back was all strapped with adhesive tape and I was ahead 3-1. I think he got a little irritated though and he took the next five games."

At this crucial point I get up and tell Tony I'm going to change my shirt which is pretty soaked. That's not why I'm getting up, though—Tony is closing in. He's going to *tell* me about the match. I can feel it. He's got all the bait out and if I don't bite he'll tell me anyway. If I say, "Nice day for the beach," again, he'll say, "Nice day to beat Delacourt."

I can't stand the thought and I take off for the locker room. As I change my shirt I keep thinking about it. Why won't I ask him? What's the matter with me? Why don't I say to Tony, "Who'd you play this morning?" Why don't I say it in front of seven of the guys? It would be around the whole club in fifteen minutes. It would be a blessing. It would be heard in Rome and Jerusalem. And when I appear at the Gates, and when they ask me what I have done, my advocate could say, "He asked Tony Mancuso in front of seven guys." And oh Lord, those gates would swing open because with thirty million tennis players this is no longer a game. This is religion.

I begin to daydream and a picture flashes across my mind. It's Mason, playing tennis on his private court in Greenwich. God, how I would have liked to grow up in Greenwich. As it happened I grew up on the streets of Brooklyn—a stickball champion. Ten years devoted to stickball. If stickball becomes the national game instead of tennis, I'll become Mason and Mason will become me.

My mind drifts from stickball to baseball, and to the bleachers of Ebbets Field. I'm sitting there between two mustache-types and feeling very uncomfortable. Suddenly Mancuso appears and hollers out a big hello. I make out like I don't see him.

I wake up and observe that my daydreams don't take much to figure out. Even my daydreams have no class. Some guys have poetic, sophisticated daydreams; you could write a book about them. My daydreams wouldn't even make the pulps.

But at least I know where I'm at, I figure. At least I know where I want to be. I want to be right here on the beaches of East Hampton—one of the loveliest places in the world. And I want to play tennis at this private club where a lot of the guys are lawyers and writers and advertising executives, and everyone is lean and sun-burned and terrific-looking. I didn't just stumble into this—it took a lot of work—it took some brains, and maybe even a measure of class. I'm here now; I'm part of this. Don't let this go, I tell myself.

It's the afternoon, and I'm lying on the beach. Ron and Peter walk over. Am I going back to the club? Do I need a ride? Of course I'm going back to the club. Where else do I spend every waking hour that I'm not on the beach?

Ron picks me up in his Mercedes and we pick up Peter. Peter's trying out a new metal racquet. We talk about metal racquets. Mason uses metal.

We reach the club and walk onto the patio. There are only two people sitting there; no one has returned from the beach yet. Larry is sitting in a far corner reading the *Times*. Tony is sitting a little closer. *Now* I'll ask him, I think. It's easy—I'll just ask him. But I can't. What the hell is this? A simple little question about who won a tennis match and I can't ask him. Tony starts to rise as we enter. He obviously thinks he's the fourth in a doubles match. Somehow we gravitate toward Larry. Tony slumps back in his chair. Larry puts down the financial section and we all go out on court one. No one else is there so we naturally take the best court. Yet there is that subtle awareness that we belong on court one.

Tony wanders over to watch. He looks so shaggy and forlorn. I'm aware of what I'm doing and I genuinely feel sorry for him. I guess I don't feel *very* sorry for him because it wouldn't take much to do something about it.

It's my serve. The first one goes into the net. Three hundred dollars in lessons from the best pro on Long Island and I still hit every first serve into the net. I get ready for my second serve and I catch Mancuso out of the corner of my eye. My mind flies back to Ebbets Field and I start to think of the hot dogs that we used to pass up the stands, hand-to-hand, overhead.

Ron hollers it's my second serve and what's the matter?

I don't know what's the matter.

I hit the second serve way past the baseline and stand there for a minute. I'm not sure what I'm feeling, but things seem to be getting a little clearer. Then I walk over and sit down next to Tony Mancuso.

He looks at me. "You O.K.?" he asks.

"A little tired," I say and put a hand on his shoulder. "Why don't you take my place?"

Tony smiles his gold-tooth smile and I start to feel better. Tomorrow I might ask him how he did against Mason.

"Great get!"

"Freddy's really into this cloning thing. He thinks he'd make a great doubles team."

"Are you ready for the all-district final, Sam?"

"Now our past champion will hand over the trophy...
please hand over the trophy!"

"Hurry up with breakfast, willya, I'll be late for my match!"

Teddy Tinling on Tour

GORDON FORBES

Teddy Tinling was possessed of a fearful forehand, a safe backhand and an extraordinary turn-of-the-century type service which necessitated a very high throw-up. While the ball was thus aloft, Teddy was able to accomplish the various maneuvers which he felt belonged to and were an essential part of his swing. When things went well and the racquet and ball rendezvoused satisfactorily, an unlikely cannon ball was produced. Windy days caused Teddy's service to be fraught with tension and often forced him to re-position himself to ensure being present when the ball returned to earth after toss-up. Scarborough, that windiest of windy places, has spawned some remarkable Tinling rhetoric. One tense morning match, for example, he had to contend not only with a gale force wind, but the sun directly in his eyes.

"The whole match got completely out of hand," he recounted, "and would have been laughable if it hadn't been so serious. In the second set, at set point for me, I threw the ball up to serve, and never saw it again! I waited tensely for some time before I realised that it wasn't going to come down, ever again!"

"What did you do?" I asked him.

"My dear chap, what *was* there to do? I simply threw up the second ball, hoping that whatever it was up there that was taking away my tennis balls, wouldn't do it again. I was so relieved when the second one came down after all, that I served a double. It's bad enough to have to serve a second ball on set point when you *know* it's coming down, but the first one *hadn't,* you see, and I wasn't sure!"

What had happened, in fact, was that Teddy had thrown the ball high into the sun and a terrific gust of wind had blown it into the hedge behind him. The match wended its way to the close, and finally Teddy was down at set point against him.

"It was his service," he said, "and when he missed his first ball, I knew I had him because he was serving into the wind. His second ball came straight towards me, and as I was getting ready to hit it, it suddenly turned off at right angles, fell on the line and went into the water jug under the umpire's chair."

"What did you do?" I asked. I was prepared to ask the most inane questions just to make him continue.

"I questioned the umpire," he said, "and made him consult the rule book. There are so many, you see—rules, I mean, and one never knows whether rule two of paragraph three might read: 'a second service on match point which finishes in a water jug may be declared a let'. But there was nothing so I had to concede."

Match points used to give Teddy tremendous problems.

"They rarely come my way," he said, "but when they do, I prepare for the worst. On grass my opponents invariably serve into a weed!"

At Eastbourne, at the end of that first season, Gordon Talbot and I found ourselves playing doubles against Teddy and Howard Walton. They both had immense forehands and positioned themselves so that it was almost impossible to hit on their backhands. We were thus confronted by streams of these forehands which we had to volley back, and having at that time limited experience, we made heavy weather of the match. We reached match point at last, and Gordon was given a short lob which he killed with terrific force. It had been raining heavily all week, and where the smash bounced, a small jet of water arose from the grass to the height of about eighteen inches.

"Great Scott!" cried Teddy, "he's opened up a spring! That's all I need—a match point against me where my opponent's smash opens a spring!"

The incident added another story to Teddy's repertoire, already colorful. And often on other occasions I heard Teddy's voice from the corner of the change-room or tea-lounge:

"—At match point with a smash so powerful it

opened up a spring on the court!"

Manchester was the first big grass court event of the season. That was the year that Teddy Tinling got to play against Lew Hoad. In those days Teddy designed tennis gear for both men and women, and, whereas in the realms of women's wear he was undoubtedly top dog, he had tremendous competition in the men's section from Fred Perry. Both strove to get the best players to wear their clothes. Perry used the green laurel wreath as his emblem, while Teddy had a sort of red rose affair (which sometimes ran into the white of the shirt). That season, to Teddy's profound delight, Hoad had agreed to wear his clothing. And in Manchester, when Teddy arrived for the tournament, he found that if he was able to win the first round, he would play Hoad (the number one seed) in the second. He was, simultaneously, ecstatic and deeply anxious. His first-round opponent was a venerable, but wily, English veteran, a Lord-someone-or-other, with whom, in those days, English tournaments abounded.

From experience in county matches, Teddy knew that he would be hard pressed to win.

"I have the better forehand, do you see," he said to me. "But Lords can be damned crafty. Play all day long, you see. Don't have to make dresses for a living."

Yet, to reach the second round, to walk onto the center court ("I'm certain to be on center, dear chap," he said to me, breathlessly) with Hoad, the pair of them dressed all in white Tinling gear, was an opportunity "too horrible to contemplate missing." By the time Teddy's first-round match was due on court, word had got round, and although it was scheduled for court seventeen or thereabouts, many players, including Hoad, went to watch. It was a typical Manchester day. Gusty wind, rain clouds hurrying across leaky skies, and British spectators opening and closing umbrellas and looking upwards at the clouds and saying: "Oh, it's bound to clear up after tea."

"Tinling to serve," the umpire called. "Players ready. Play!"

Teddy got the ball well and truly airborne with his

left hand, while his right, attached to the handle of his racquet, began the devious swing which would, if things went according to plan, bring the head of his racquet round in a final sweep to meet the ball on its downward journey. From the very outset, it was clear that the elements were against him. The wind was whistling directly down court so that serving against it, Teddy found himself bent over backwards like a bow, while with it, he would be leaning far in court, struggling to keep his feet in contact with the fair territory behind the baseline while hitting the ball without falling flat on his face immediately afterwards.

With the business of serving over, play became very brisk. Teddy effectively brought his forehand to bear, directing his shots to his opponent's backhand. His opponent, meanwhile, had a good crosscourt backhand, which he employed to get the ball back to Teddy's backhand side, forcing him farther and farther over to the left. Extraordinary reverse crosscourt rallies developed.

"I spent more than half the match with my backside interfering with play on the court next door," said Teddy later.

Occasionally, diabolical down-the-line direction changes kept both players on tenterhooks. It was a desperate, even encounter.

At set and 4-5 Teddy found himself down 30-40, match point on his own service, with the wind behind him and still rising. To make matters even more difficult, just at that moment a series of terrific gusts shook the court, causing Teddy to miss with his first service. His toss-up had blown so far over to the northwest that he had nearly pulled a muscle getting within striking distance. He paused then, and stood scowling at the one remaining ball in his hand, waiting for the wind to abate. It wouldn't. A tense hush fell. His first toss-up with the second ball blew so far into the court that he walked after it and caught it. This happened three times. On the fourth attempt, Teddy, by now desperate, stepped into the court after the ball, gave it a desperate whack, and served an unlikely and extraordinary ace. Everyone, including Teddy himself, was dumbstruck. A footfault call seemed inevitable, but none came.

"Deuce," called the umpire.

"My dear fellow," said Teddy's opponent, "surely that was a —, I mean to say, surely that was a — well, you know, well, surely —? Mr. Umpire, do you wish to call a footfault?"

"Deuce," repeated the umpire with a stoicism achieved only by umpires who are convinced that they are correct.

"Mr. Umpire," persisted the peer, "do you wish to call a footfault?"

"Deuce," called the umpire.

"Mr. Umpire—" began the peer again.

"I *do not* wish to call a footfault," said the umpire flatly. "The score is deuce."

"That's hardly cricket," cried the peer.

"My dear chap, I quite agree," said Teddy. "After what we've been through, I can't imagine a purer conclusion."

"It appeared to be a footfault."

"I can't comment because I was busy at the time," said Teddy. "Besides, I had nothing to do with the whole incident. In order to hit the ball, I was forced to station myself in the area in which I expected it to descend. An unfair advantage couldn't have been further from my intentions!"

In my opinion, this probably rates as one of the purest tennis arguments in history. Teddy won the match, and took the center court amidst cheers the next afternoon to play Lew Hoad. Teddy lost 6-0, 6-0. Afterwards, in the dressing-room, he said excitedly:

"I was *mentally* prepared for the match, but mental ability alone was useless. To begin with, one needs to face oneself in the right direction. I spent half the match hitting backhands with my forehand grip, and forehands with my backhand grip. Lew was very polite. He'd call out to me: 'Are you ready, Teddy?', and I'd call back that I was, but I wasn't. Not once in the entire match was I ready!"

"Will you be doing any typing today, Miss Fletcher?"

"Offhand, I'd say he ran around his backhand once too often."

On Court with the Beautiful People

**ART
BUCHWALD**

Since very few people have had an opportunity to play tennis with the Kennedys at Hyannisport, I thought I would tell you what it's like.

The Kennedys, all of them, play a very wicked, fast, skillful and psychological game—mostly psychological.

Their strategy is to make you feel inferior when you come on the court and keep you that way until the match is over.

This is how a typical game goes. And I wish to say right now I have no reason to exaggerate.

Let us say that a doubles game has been arranged with Ethel Kennedy and her sister-in-law Jean Smith on one side, and you and a houseguest on the other.

You arrive for the game and go out on the court to warm up. The first thing Ethel says is, "You're not going to play in those dirty white sneakers are you?"

"They're not that dirty," you protest.

"We play in whites on this court and that includes footwear."

You start rubbing your sneakers against your wool socks, hoping to get some of the dirt off.

No luck. You begin to warm up. You hit one into the net.

Jean Smith says, "Oh for God's sakes. I thought we came to play tennis."

"It's just a volley," you point out.

"The idea," Ethel says, "is to get it over the net."

You haven't even started yet and already you're shaking with fear.

After a five-minute warmup someone says "Let's serve."

Ethel twirls her racquet. "Rough or smooth?"

"Smooth," I say.

"Rough it is," she shouts back. No one ever gets to inspect a Kennedy's racquet when twirling for serve.

The game begins. Ethel serves and you return it with a lob, which she hits over the fence.

"If you're going to lob, why don't we call it quits now," she says bitterly. "That's not tennis."

You make a mental note not to lob.

The game continues with either Jean Smith or Ethel making a comment on each point.

Jean Smith on occasion hits the ball so hard it goes through the fence without touching the ground. Then she says innocently, "Was that in?"

Ethel hits one three feet out. You say "No good.'

Ethel turns to a spectator. "Do you mind calling them? He's blind."

On the other hand, when you hit one into the backcourt, either one of them shouts "OUT" before the ball even has a chance to bounce.

Ethel hates opponents who play the net. One of her favorite shots is to aim the ball right at the net player's face. If she succeeds and the opponent falls to the ground holding his eye, she runs up and says, "Oh I'm terribly sorry. I didn't mean to do that."

"That's all right," you say, bravely smiling. "I should have had my racquet up."

The thing you must remember when you play tennis with the Kennedys is that they hate to lose. If, with all the gamesmanship they use, you still beat them, they insist on playing another set. If you win that one they insist on a third.

The safest thing to do if you want to have dinner is to play well but lose. Otherwise you'll be out on the court all night.

I'll never regret having played tennis with the Kennedys. I can honestly say that everything I know about the game I have learned from them. Just the other day I was playing at a friend's court in Washington, and on the return I hit the ball up and broke a window on the second floor of the house.

I immediately said to the owner, "Was that out?"

Ethel would've been proud of me.

House Guest 40, Host 0

DAVID WILTSE

It is Sunday afternoon and a great experiment in tennis paternalism is about to begin. My wife, Nancy, and I have volunteered to feed and shelter one of the players who will be competing in a big 21-and-under tournament at the nearby Four Seasons Racquet Club in Wilton, Conn. That is, I volunteered after the club posted an appeal in the lobby for player housing and then had to come on like a carpet salesman to convince Nancy what a noble and worthwhile act it would be.

Now, while all right-minded citizens are out playing tennis, we are at home, waiting most of the day to find out who, and where, our guest is.

McEnroe did this, I reflect. Tanner, Gottfried, Solomon and all the rest of them did it, too, traveling across the country at a tender age, boarding with strangers. I expect someone lean and hungry; maybe spitting and brash like Connors; or maybe soulful like Vilas, reading poetry in his room. But in any event, someone who's ready and willing to kill himself for success.

Nancy will give him spirtual comfort, the security of a good home. I will refine his game with a few subtle, but perceptive, changes and he will acknowledge my help when he accepts the trophy. If only Connors had enjoyed the benefit of my guidance at a similar age, maybe he wouldn't have such a problem with his forehand approach shot today.

I wisely mention none of these musings to my wife, who is concerned only with whether he is housebroken. Will he help out or think that the world owes him a living because he plays tennis?

She scurries around tidying the house and the kids. I refuse to be tidied. "Relax," I say. "He's only a kid." She shoots me her withering, you-can-be-such-a-fool look and goes on picking up the debris of living.

He finally arrives and I surreptitiously tuck in my shirt. Our two small girls hide behind my legs. He says he didn't get in touch earlier because he had to win three rounds to qualify for housing. That has a nice elitist ring to it. This house for winners only.

His name is Mike and he's from Beverly Hills, Calif. He will be entering Harvard in the fall. Beverly Hills? Harvard? Where's my lean and needy gladiator?

After introducing himself, he allows as how he's "kind of hungry." Methusaleh was kind of old. The boy eats like a ravenous bear after a particularly long winter. Nancy takes one look at the way he's chowing down and hides the cats.

SUNDAY NIGHT

We've found out a bit about our young man. His father is a Beverly Hills doctor who has made a killing in real estate. I assume that his specialty is removing swollen wallets; he'd have to be rich to handle his son's food bill.

Mike browses through my books, confessing that he's "kind of heavily into reading." I don't know what that means, but he adds: "I've seen a lot of these books around." Are my tastes too common for him?

Nancy wishes our house was bigger, grander. She figures that at home he probably has the East Wing to himself. At our house, he's sleeping on a rented bed in the room I use for an office. I try to assuage Nancy's feelings of being judged.

"He's only a kid," I say. "Kids don't notice things like houses."

We hear a low, scraping, shuffling sound from downstairs. "The raccoons are at the garbage again," says Nancy. I investigate and find Mike in the kitchen, rummaging through the cabinets, making himself at home and searching for a snack.

MONDAY

Learned a bit more about Mike this morning. At the age of 14, he was ranked No. 9 nationally in singles in his age group and No. 2 in doubles. He's only 17 now and playing up. For a time, he was debating whether to do the tour this season and finally decided that he might as well: "I told my parents that earning a wage during the summer would just be a farce, anyway."

I remember doing farm labor for 35 cents an hour when I was his age. If I'd told my father it was a farce, he would have had me doing it for 25 cents an hour just to tone down my sense of humor. On the other hand, I was never No. 2 in the country at anything.

The rest of my family doesn't suffer from the hangover of a Nebraska upbringing and they don't share my resentment. "Remember, people from Beverly Hills are as much in need of understanding as anyone else," says Nancy. I have been to Beverly Hills and I have my doubts. But I hold my tongue.

Lisa, my 2-year-old, is flirting unconscionably with Mike without getting the slightest acknowledgement. Laura, at 5, is more subtle. She pretends he isn't around, referring to him in the third person when he's sitting next to her.

"Daddy," she says, "I have a secret." I lean over to hear.

"How long is he going to stay?" she booms out in a voice that carries for blocks.

Mike has his own version of tact. "Those kids are really going to be spoiled when they get older," he tells Nancy. "You'd better get a grip on them while you can."

I quickly restrain Nancy. One more remark like that and she'll have a contract out on him by morning.

"How was your bed?" I say, changing the subject. "I've slept in better," says Mike. "But it was O.K."

"It was probably the pea under the mattress," I say. No one laughs.

With some trepidation, I offer him my battered Toyota to get to and from the tournament. He allows as how it's really neat—for such an old car. He wouldn't want to have to drive his dad's Mercedes on all the narrow winding roads around here.

"Yeah, that's why I didn't get a Mercedes," I mutter.

"This was all your idea!" Nancy roars when we're alone. "He disapproves of everything!"

"I hadn't noticed," I lie. But I'm concerned. It's certainly not working out the way I planned.

I practice with Mike before his first match. He is really good! His backhand booms like Vilas' and he volleys like Gottfried. He's got the same forehand weakness as Connors, but I'll soon take care of that. "This kid can take the whole thing," I decide proudly.

Things start to slide back into perspective. He's here to play tennis, not to be adopted. He probably feels just as awkward and uncomfortable as we do. But what a backhand!

TUESDAY

Gloom and Despond. Mike lost in the first round of the singles 6-4, 6-4. He got over his subsequent depression by practicing for three hours in 90-degree heat and 90-percent humidity.

He arrives in time for dinner, however. Nancy cooked a chicken for our family and another chicken for Mike. It wasn't quite enough, but he filled up on bread.

After dinner, Mike asks if there's a scale around. I tell him there's one in the bathroom. "Oh, does that one work? It looks broken."

He's worried about his weight! I could suggest a way he might control it, but I still hold my peace. Besides, he spoke to the girls tonight, smiled at Lisa's antics and even mentioned how cute they are. There is no quicker way to a parent's heart. The ice is beginning to thaw a bit.

TUESDAY NIGHT

A local player stops by to see Mike tonight. Nancy answers the door and the young lout asks if she is my daughter. "Yeah, she really looks young, doesn't she?" Mike says.

Nancy is flying. The entire visit has been justified. "It was all your idea," she reminds me as I examine my horribly aged face in the mirror. Nancy is only five years younger than I am.

"My daughter?" I exclaim. "My *daughter*?!"

"It was dark, he couldn't really see me," Nancy says without conviction, peeking into the mirror at herself. I'm considering a facelift. She's grinning at herself. "Remember, he's only a kid," she says in a disgustingly youthful voice.

She and Mike are suddenly fast friends. They spend

two hours later in the evening talking over the kitchen table, exchanging life histories. Well, kids will be kids. They have so much in common.

WEDNESDAY
Mike has his first doubles match, teamed with a bean-pole-thin California friend.(*This* kid's not eating any-one out of house and home.)

The friend has a great deal of touch, Mike hits with power. They make a great team. Hey, I realize, these guys could go all the way!

My guys win in a third-set tiebreaker from an older, more experienced team. No extra practice today.

After his victory, Mike is positively expansive. I ask him how his experience has been so far.

"The housing gets an A," he says. "It's the little extras that make the difference, like the car and the fan in the room." I'm beginning to like this kid.

Mike tells me he has been on the national circuit since he was 11 years old. His family stopped traveling with him when he was 14. "Every year I get a little braver," he says. "I learn more about different places and people, I do more things for myself. And every housing is different. For instance, you're the first one with little kids." I always knew my children would make me memorable.

Then, he tells a story about a 30-year-old widow who provided housing once. It sounds a little bit like the traveling salesman and the farmer's daughter to me, filled with wishful teenage hyperbole. But it does make me wonder fleetingly why Nancy insisted that we have a young man rather than a young woman.

The Four Seasons has a barbecue dinner for play-ers and hosts. Mike is very eager about the second round of doubles tomorrow. If he wins twice more, he'll get an automatic exemption for the next tourna-ment and won't have to qualify. Because of the tension, he limits himself to four helpings of barbecue, three soft drinks and three desserts.

THURSDAY
They've put my boy's match on the least visible court. I sense a conspiracy here, feeling as paranoid as any

tennis parent. His opponents are brothers from Chile, huge topspinners. Mike and his partner take off like the surf is up, streaking to a 5-1 lead.

I'm bouncing around, delighted, pointing to Mike and saying "that's my boy" to anyone who will listen. Then, the roof caves in. The Chileans get their topspin grooved and catch up, then take the tiebreaker. My boys are up a break in the second, but ultimately lose that one, too.

Gloom and Despond. Mike hits balls the rest of the afternoon.

Nancy ventures into Mike's room while he's practicing and finds a large, pulsating mass in one corner. It's his dirty laundry. The fumes are beginning to peel off the wallpaper.

"This was all your idea," she reminds me yet again. I wash his laundry.

Suddenly, Mike is gone, off to New York to see a friend, then to Pennsylvania for the next tournament. We feel a bit strange, as if some part of us has been unceremoniously uprooted.

"It's good to have a guest every now and then; it forces you to re-examine yourself," Nancy says.

My 2-year-old wanders around, looking lost. "Michael?" she calls. "Michael gone?"

"Why did he leave so soon?" Laura wants to know.

"Hey," I tell everyone, trying to cheer them up. "He was only a kid!" Fortunately, he's promised to come back next year.

Tennis with Ustinov

GORDON FORBES

When I was younger I used to day-dream quite a lot. I still do, but not nearly so much—because, I suppose, day-dreams are the inventions of young minds which, when they are older, have used up many of the dreams and found them empty; and, if they are very lucky, have made one or two come true. I am not sure whether Rod Laver ever day-dreamed. If he did, one of his dreams came true that Wimbledon. Not that he surprised anyone by winning the tournament—simply that it was his first Wimbledon victory and, as I have said somewhere before, the particular moment of that victory must rate as the great thrill of a tennis lifetime, even one as illustrious as Laver's.

I became very friendly with Rodney during that Wimbledon as he was very fond of my sister, Jean, and we spent a good deal of time together. And also Peter Ustinov, who used to love to watch the matches and who amused the devil out of us by his remarks and observations. In an animated monologue he could carry out an altercation between, say, an Italian player, a French player, a British umpire and a sleeping woman linesman and sort the whole thing out after a heated argument. On the evening of the Friday on which Rodney won his title, we went to Peter's show, *Romanoff and Juliet,* which, like many of his shows, cut into the heart of human affairs and dressed up the wound in nonsense. Rod took a bow during the show when Peter called the spotlights onto him, and afterwards we drank beer at the *Down Under Club.*

Later that year when we arrived at Istanbul for the tournament in Turkey, I heard that Peter was in that extraordinary city making a film called *Topkapi* which was about a robbery of jewels from the Sultan's palace, or something like that. At any rate, there was a great deal of running around on the turrets and roof-tops of some famous building, and laughter in the making. Peter invited some of us to watch the filming of one of his scenes and in return we asked him to the tennis. He duly arrived, together with Max Schell who co-starred in the film. In the evening, when it was cooler, I asked him whether he would like to play a game or two. We found some gear and went down to one of the back courts, where we began our hit-up.

Peter can best be described as a determined and well-anchored player. His forehand comes out from around his middle, the racquet head gaining speed all the time, so that by the time contact is made, a shot of considerable velocity is produced. The fact that it sometimes flies off course, like a spark off a catherine wheel, is probably due to the fact that he doesn't practice as much as he should. His backhand is a more modest shot—a short-arm jab, struck with a sulky frown. Mobility is also a problem.

"Getting oneself into position is like moving troops," he once said. "One has to plan well in advance!"

He kept referring to himself as "one." "One should lose weight if one wants to indulge in this sport." Or: "One must watch the ball. Even if one can't get to it, one should at least *watch* it!"

Max Schell sat on a bench at the side of the court, chuckling away to himself. Peter frowned at him periodically and gave him his famous sulky looks.

"One doesn't like being laughed at," he said. "Especially by *German* spectators. One would expect them to remain silent during play."

Our warm-up reached the stage where I felt we should play a few games. Peter looked exceedingly dubious at my suggestion.

"Do you mean actually *compete*?" he asked with his mouth turning right down at the corners. "Score points? One isn't accustomed to actual athletic confrontation you know. Damned alarming when you meet it face to face! Oh very well. But you serve first. Then one shall be able to say that, 'games went with service in the early stages!' "

I held my service and we changed ends. Peter gathered the balls and himself together and took up his position on the serving line, standing there like a bewildered Roman commander who is not sure what has become of his armies. For a few moments he stood glancing from the racquet in his right hand to the balls in his left, as if wondering which to toss up. I stood waiting, half expecting him to put on some kind of show—an impersonation perhaps, of some famous player's service action. Instead, he began a sort of flouncing and curtseying action, his racquet going back in a series of little loops and frills, one to the front, one to the side and one behind him, while his eyes followed the racquet head and his knees bobbed up and down in anticipating bends, as though they had not been told which twirl was to lead to the final swing.

Suddenly, while all this maneuvering was taking place, his left hand, activated by some extraordinary and complex timing system, threw a ball about ten feet into the air above his head where it performed a graceful little parabola before beginning its descent. I, meanwhile, watched open-mouthed and just as I had decided that there was no earthly way that this preposterous swing would ever unravel itself in time to hit the ball, a racquet head came flying out of the tangle and gave the ball a crisp whack which sent it whistling past me about knee height without a bounce.

"Good God!" I exclaimed, convinced now that Peter was doing some elaborate send-up of, perhaps, a turn-of-the-century ladies' doubles serve. No one in their right mind, I decided, would consider such a service as standard equipment. "That's the funniest service I've ever seen," I called. "Do another one!"

"One has to," said Peter. "It's the only service one has!"

Hearing funny noises at the side of the court, I turned to find that Max Schell had fallen off his seat and was rolling with laughter. Peter frowned at both of us, sniffed and muttered something about it being "very difficult to concentrate on one's game when the stands were full of unruly spectators."

On finals day, Peter and Max Schell played a set of mixed doubles on the center court, partnered by Margaret Hunt and Annette van Zyl, and by that time I had alerted some of the players to take note of Peter's service action. His first service game was thus greeted by cheers from the players' enclosure and near hysteria by the spectators.

"I seem," said Peter to his partner, "to be some kind of Turkish Delight!"

It's Not Love But it's Not Bad

RICHARD R. SZATHMARY

Reaching down from the wooden bleachers at courtside at such an acute angle that the "F" on the Fila chest patch on his tennis shirt upends itself into a rune, he taps the woman with the flat of his Arthur Ashe Comp 2, in a modern chivalric gesture, and asks the classic singles question:

"Do you come here often?"

She turns to look up on this chilly Friday night, letting her hot orange-and-white cardigan fall off her shoulder so he can see she's wearing a Mondessa dress with straps that sit in close on the neckline and expose a lot of epidermis.

"We'll, I'm not a regular here, if that's what you mean."

He's gratified. "That's what I meant. I've never seen you here before. The two times I've been here myself previous to this one, of course."

"Of course, right." She smiles warmly, adjusts the cardigan.

He hesitates. "Ah, do you have a partner for the mixed doubles yet?"

"No, that is, my friend, well, you know...she's been here before, she's met somebody she already knew."

"I know." He nods sagely. "That settles it then?" She nods back.

Raising his racquet up in the air, he catches the eye of one of the house pros, who's been writing players' names on index cards and separating them into two piles—male and female.

"We've just accomplished a pairing here," the guy with the Comp 2 yells.

The pro grins, puts his cards down. "Hey," he

shouts, "hey, hey. Another match." He's the host of the Gong Show, or maybe chubbily dim Merv Griffin when he doesn't have the slightest idea what a guest is up to. "Another dynamic duo formed, people. Now who says you won't have a ripping time tonight, huh? Who says?" It's a dare and nobody present says.

The pro chuckles to himself, smacks his fists together in satisfaction, rubs his outrageously rosy cheeks. Then he looks up at the rest of us, still to his great personal shame *unpaired* and *unmatched,* and momentarily loses his toothy smile as he commiserates with us. Fila and Mondessa have started to rally together on a nearby court. All eyes are enviously on them; like the pro says. "They make a handsome couple." It's like clock watching during a particularly slow-passing homeroom detention back in high school on a rainy day when you'd really rather be home watching "American Bandstand."

Fila and Mondessa stop play. "We need some company," Fila says to the pro. "Send us over some more players." Mondessa seconds with: "We're ready if they are."

And the pro snaps to attention and salutes them back. He is clearly very aware of his matchmaking responsibilities—and he should be.

Among indoor tennis center management people, like the operators of this particular 12-court complex, the big thing lately is to "go singles." It's like staking out a claim to your own piece of the rock, the rock in this case being that attractively free-spending and unattached group of men and women, ages perhaps 22 to 35, who'd like to meet members of the opposite sex in an ostensibly "pressureless" situation, as the classified ads in papers like the Village Voice and Boston Phoenix sometimes put it. Tie this biological necessity into the glamour and growth sport of tennis and you've got a powerful combination.

Besides, "going singles" alleviates a common problem at indoor tennis centers on Friday and Saturday nights—the fact that they tend to be as busy as Forest Hills in February. "I was stuck," club owner Otto states.

He explains how on Friday and Saturday nights he'd formerly book anything to earn some money. "Bar mitzvahs. Married suburbanites who just want to get sloshed together over tennis. Kiwanis meetings." He's even allowed an on-court wedding.

Then, Otto laces his fingers together in thoughtful repose. "Ah, but the singles, my singles are my weekend bread and butter . . . My singles don't even care if I overbook a smidgen. Sure, it means less tennis for them than the two hours we 'guarantee,' but it also means more courtside socializing. And the one thing I've learned from this business is that less is more."

The problem sometimes lies in deciding how much less constitutes how much more. Upstairs on the night I'm there, for instance, at least 50 persons dressed in tennis clothes are sampling Otto's buffet and hanging around the bar. Most of them—unlike Fila, Mondessa and myself—never even bother to register with the house pro for "matches." And I doubt that many of them ever get downstairs to actually hit a tennis ball.

When I ask a red-headed woman in a lacy tennis dress whether she intends to play, she shrugs and says: "You get what you pay for."

O.K., what then has she paid for?

"The chance to learn that that beautiful Greek god over there with the layer cut is a guy I used to go out with who's lost 25 pounds, started using good French cologne and lost my phone number after he went on his diet but nevertheless wanted me to be the first to know. And don't think that I don't love knowing."

I wouldn't think of it.

It's time to check out the buffet. The chopped liver is in the shape of a giant tennis ball, resting on a racquet made out of a loaf of French bread (the handle) and a circular seeded loaf (the head) and an intricate tracery of mini-breadsticks (the strings). A platter of tripe in tomato sauce is advertised by a sign that reads "Home-cooked gut." The green gelatin salad, with chick-peas and nuts folded in, similarly sports a titled card of "Fresh made, cold Har-Tru." This is the bestial level of imagery the advertising world has inflicted on the

American mind. Even the cold cuts are arranged in strips to look like tri-colored wristbands.

Standing there, I pick up snatches of conversation that are instantaneous one-act plays:

"Oh, I like a girl with a good backhand all right, but when her arm looks like Rod Laver's, it's time to split."

"But if I go home with you this early, then I'm out all that money."

"No, you do not use the Australian formation in mixed doubles. You want everybody else here to think we have dirty minds?"

"Of course I write my real name in on the cards for the draw. I also write in my town. It never hurts to at least let a cute pro know you're in the book."

"I don't know why I bother to keep running into you. You don't like drinking beer, you don't like Sam Peckinpah movies and you're useless to me against spin. And don't talk about love, not when my game is so off."

"Sure he's an idiot. I know that. I knew it when I saw him wearing argyle socks on court. But he's got the money to buy a Tony Trabert C-6 and that shows me something else about him."

"Listen, if we're serious about this relationship, we're going to have to practice before next Saturday. I suggest we go home now and meet tomorrow at dawn on the public courts."

"Aaaaaahhhh, a blister on my index finger. I knew I shouldn't have fiddled around with an American twist tonight."

"I'd ask your name, but what if it turns out we already know each other? We might even be cousins or something. Does incest count in doubles?"

Suddenly, however, all bitterness in the air disappears from the room as Fila and Mondessa walk in— holding hands. They approach the buffet table, pick up one plate between them and drop a little spinach salad with bacon and a few meatballs on it. Then, they walk quietly over to a corner where they nibble ever so daintily.

There are sighs of envy. There is also the house pro

standing in the doorway, beaming. "I come up for a sandwich," he says with a note of wonder in his voice, "and what I get instead is a snapshot of my prize match of the evening getting it on."

Is it ever thus so romantic?

Anna shakes her head: "I've been going to these things, when I could afford them, for two years now. You can have a good time but it's always one or the other—good socializing or else good tennis. They rarely coincide."

She's tapped on the shoulder. She turns and faces a tall, thin man with a downright Satanic, fork-shaped beard, wearing a Tacchini shirt whose vivid bloodied hue only enforce the smell of brimstone about him. Even his racquet is jet black, the strings possessed of an unsettling matte finish.

"I couldn't help noticing your strawberries," he opens. Anna's wearing a special appliqued top and a pair of shorts similarly decorated. She waits.

"And I was just thinking," Satan continues, "how nice it would be if it turned out that your heart also was shaped like a strawberry."

Anna remains silent.

He wants to play doubles with her and he extends his racquet to her, head first. "Come, please. Come and join me." Although his voice is gracious, his racquet seems to have assumed a life of its own in Anna's eyes, like a piece of forbidden fruit. Later, she'll even claim that "It was pulsating!"

She finally gets out a nervous "No thanks, I'm busy."

"Pity," the man replies. "I only hope you'll realize that someday."

Later, I see that, whatever aura of the pit he carries, this guy also has some cool, if cool derived from old Bela Lugosi and George Zucco flicks. Because he's somehow got the sole awesomely beautiful woman here to play with him.

I ask the male half of a couple they defeat what it'd been like. "Like playing against Svengali and Trilby," he replies with a shudder. "I was afraid to win. I had to keep reminding my partner not to rush the net. I got the distinct feeling that guy doesn't take losing pleasantly at all."

As the evening tails off, the lights are turned off on various courts no longer in use. People begin heading for the lockers. The mysterious stranger in the blood red Tacchini shirt is seen to give his spellbound consort a peck on the forehead before reassuring her that he'll be back soon.

So he opens the door leading to the men's locker room, turning to give a big wave to everybody watching him. On his face is what 19th century Gothic writers used to call a "risus sardonicus," a smile that looks unnaturally affixed. Then, he kind of slips into the mists raised by the thundering showers that waft out over the courts.

People just start. "I wouldn't have believed it if I hadn't seen it," an assistant house pro says. "What do you want to bet that if we go in after him he's not there?" Nobody buys the challenge.

Then, there's Cecile. In blouse and skirt, she seems harmless, vulnerable. Even before heading for the locker room, she meekly assents to doubles with a beefy, mustached stockbroker named Chet who has the habit of standing in shadows whenever possible so he can show off his expensive Japanese digital watch to best advantage.

But when Cecile hits the court to play, it's like the transformation from Queen to Wicked Witch in "Snow White." The pink ribbon is gone from her hair, which is now lank and greasy like Rosemary Casals', replaced by a beaded headband. Her socks are the thick woolen kind. She wears shorts and a T-shirt with the VIVA logo. She holds her racquet like a club. The total effect is a tennis version of Boadicea, the queen of pre-historic Britain who took up shield and axe to drive the Roman legions from her country.

And Chet isn't in her league. Playing like the cantankerous Molly Volley in "Peanuts" who so dismays Snoopy with her aggression, Cecile is all over the court, chopping recklessly away. Once she even swats through Chet's legs for a ball as he merely tries to back away. The couple on the other side of the net isn't prepared for an opponent who calls every serve of theirs "out by at least a foot." Chet can't hack a partner who calls him a "macho lardass" because he doesn't bend down far enough for half-volleys.

When they come off the court, after winning 6-3,6-1, Chet is in bad shape.

"It was brutal out there," he says. "I was expecting something like celebrity tennis, hit, giggle, up to Tony Trabert for an explication of that stroke. But that woman..." He starts coughing nervously. His own headband momentarily becomes a crown of thorns.

Cecile will have none of it. "I didn't show up to waste 15 bucks to play patty-cake. We've got another match in an hour, and you better be ready. Understand, hero?"

Chet shakes his head.

"Can't handle a real woman? Think we're all supposed to be weak and defenseless? I should have known there'd be trouble when you wouldn't let me buy you a drink before we played."

Two hours later, Cecile leaves with a house pro. She looks good again. Her hair has regained its sheen, picking up highlights from a pink ribbon.

Chet is still playing with his watch and telling his new, more reserved doubles partner that he'll take everything hit hard at the net and all lobs, "so you can save your strength for ground strokes, sugar."

She agrees with obvious devotion. They both looked very happy playing the sex roles that Cecile had upset earlier.

As the evening winds down, Fila and Mondessa—unsurprisingly—go off together. They are so plainly entranced with each other that they ignore everyone else's smirking and elbow nudging. Out in the parking lot, they even exchange pieces of paper with each other's phone numbers, a gesture that remains universal whether in high school gyms or singles bars.

Maybe it's the start of something, maybe it isn't. But after they've left, the house pro looks around and shouts: "Yeehoo, boys and girls! Look out for Friday and Saturday night singles tennis parties. Like Merle Haggard said in a song, 'It's not love, but it's not bad.'"

The guy is enthusiastic, you have to give him that. Anyway, as he and Fila and Mondessa already know, singles tennis parties may not always involve love, but they're still not bad. Not bad at all.

"Mine!" "Mine!"

No.1 – for a Week

BARRY TARSHIS

"Being No. 1 puts a lot of pressure on you. Everybody is always gunning for you. Every time you go out to play a match you feel as if you have to protect something. Even so, it's better than being No. 2."

—Rod Laver

For two days last summer—two glorious days, I might add—I had a chance to experience firsthand what it's like being top dog at a tennis club. Numero Uno. What is so important about having such an experience, you ask? A good question, and I can best answer it by repeating here a conversation that once took place between a late uncle of mine and my mother.

My uncle, a musician, had just returned from playing a wedding that obviously had cost the bride's parents a small fortune, and he was wondering aloud what it would be like to be that rich.

"Archie," said my mother, forever the philosophical pragmatist, "It's just like everything else."

"You don't understand," my uncle replied. "I know what everything else is like. I want to know what being rich is like."

As my uncle did, I know what "everything else" is like—in tennis. I am, I like to think, a respectable club player. My strokes aren't bad, I can move pretty well and every once in a while I can put together a string of shots so brilliant that if you happened to be watching me at that minute, you would be convinced that I was the genuine article: a blue-chip player in every way.

But let's not get carried away. If it was my job to sign up future champions for a tennis manufacturing company, I would not select myself, not even for sentimental reasons. I am not, as they say, "championship timber," and my record shows it. Prior to last summer, I had entered maybe a dozen or so club and press tournaments throughout the course of my seven-year tennis career, and the best I could show for my efforts was a runner-up trophy won in a "B" tournament in which there were only eight entries to begin with, three of whom were rank beginners and one of whom competed despite a sprained ankle that forced him to hobble around the court as if he had only one leg.

All of which is another way of saying that being acknowledged as the "best" player around is not a role to which I had become accustomed before last summer; nor is it a role I expect to assume ever again. Not that I'm complaining. To paraphrase Tennyson: "It is better to have been No. 1 and lost than never to have been No. 1 at all."

It happened at Gray Rocks, a resort in the Laurentian Mountains 75 miles outside of Montreal. I went there with my family last summer not because I was itching for tennis combat but because Gray Rocks met all of our qualifications for a "family vacation." It was located in a part of the world we'd never been to, it had good tennis possibilities, it catered to families and it had a lot of things to do apart from tennis.

I did not know at the time I made the preliminary arrangements that Gray Rocks staged guest tournaments as part of its weekly schedule. But even if I had known that, it wouldn't have made any difference. My most recent tournament experience had been so disastrous—I averaged three double faults a service game—that I had made a vow never to subject myself to organized competition again. The ego punishment was too severe.

The fact that I had made such a vow did not create any conflict at Gray Rocks, once I learned of the weekly tournament. Like a growing number of resorts, Gray Rocks has in its tennis pro shop a combination rating guide and sign-up sheet, whereby a player, by reading certain descriptions on the guide, assigns himself a numerical rating from 1.5 to 5 and puts this rating down beside his name. On the basis of the guide, I figured myself as 3.5, and when I saw the sign-up board filled with 4's and 4.5's and 5's I wasn't in the least upset about not signing up for the tournament, figuring I didn't have a chance anyway.

I changed my mind after my match with a university professor from upstate New York named Jim. I vaguely recalled seeing Jim's name on the sign-up sheet when we introduced ourselves to one another outside the pro shop, but I didn't remember his rating and certainly wasn't about to ask him about it. He was an aggressive player, deadly at the net, but not too steady, and I beat him—correction, he beat himself— without much trouble 6-2, 6-1.

"I'm curious," he said after we'd finished. "How did you rate yourself on the guide?"

"About 3.5," I said.

He frowned. "I guess," he said slowly, "that I'm not really at 4.5, am I?"

I will spare you the details of the tournaments. Yes, I said tournaments, plural. I entered the men's doubles with Jim and we won. I also entered the mixed doubles with my wife, and we won. A couple of the mixed doubles matches my wife and I played were reasonably close but, all in all, my two triumphs left little doubt in the minds of nearly everybody who took part, and watched, that I was the best player in the house. No. 1.

Now will I tell you what happens when you get to be No. 1.

First of all, the attitude of the young people who work in the pro shop changes. Pro shop personnel exercise more power than you might imagine, particularly when it comes to assigning you to a specific court. At every resort and most clubs, there are what might be called "show" or "No. 1" courts, and I can count on one hand the number of times I've played on one. I don't know exactly why, but people in charge of court assignments usually permit only the "best" players to play on certain courts. I can remember at one place one summer requesting the No. 1 court, which was empty at the time.

"I ... can't give it to you," the girl behind the counter said.

"Why?" I asked. "It's empty."

"Well," she explained with obvious uneasiness. "We have to water it now."

"But it's a concrete court," I said. "Who waters concrete courts?"

"No," she quickly said. "It's not that we have to water it, it's..."

"I know what it is," I said. "Certain courts are restricted to certain players, aren't they? *Aren't* they?" I felt like Gregory Peck in the movie "Gentlemen's Agreement."

"Listen," she pleaded. "I'm sorry. I really am. I just work here. I don't make the rules. If it was up to me, I'd let you play. Honest. Look. Why don't I give you court 14? You'll like it. It's very private. You'll be happier there."

I can't say for certain whether such a prejudicial policy exists at Gray Rocks, but I can tell you that on the two days that followed my tournament wins, I played every match on the front court.

Something else, too. During the first part of the week, the pretty young girl behind the pro shop counter had always greeted me with a smile that was friendly enough but went no further — if you know what I mean. This situation changed after I'd established my reputation. On the very afternoon of my second doubles win, in fact, when I went into the pro shop to sign up for a court, I detected a glint of something beyond common courtesy in her eyes. "Maybe later on," she said quietly, "if your wife doesn't mind, we can rally. I can get a court."

Don't worry, fans. I wasn't about to let one day of triumph ruin 14 years of marriage.

Another thing that changed once the tournament was over was the attitude of the other players at Gray Rocks. If you play tennis, you need not be reminded that tennis players—good ones, especially — can be awfully clannish. I can remember when I started playing tennis at the public courts in the town where I used to live, I would ask one of the "regulars" if he felt like hitting and he would invariably say something like: "Gee, Barry, that's a nice idea, but, I tell you, I'm really bushed, you know. I couldn't even pick up a racquet, you know what I mean?" Ten minutes later I would see him playing singles with another "regular."

At Gray Rocks, at the beginning of the week, other players simply issued invitations to me, but after the tournament, they were not so forward. "Uh, Barry," one of my opponents in the men's doubles finally said to me Thursday afternoon. "We—that is, two other guys and me—have this court in 15 minutes — and . . . I mean, it's not a *great* game or anything like that, but it might be fun, you know, if you could . . . maybe . . . uh, fill in, I mean if you don't have anything else to do."

"Gee, Phil," I remember saying. "That's a nice idea, but I tell you, I'm really bushed. I couldn't even pick up a racquet, if you know what I mean." Ten minutes later, Jim and I were playing singles.

But the biggest change of all was in me—specifically the way I handled myself on and off the court. Psychologists are forever telling us that we tend to behave in ways consistent with our self-image, and I never realized how true this was in relation to tennis until my experience at Gray Rocks.

I am not blessed with what might be called "good match temperament." When I start to miss shots, I do my best to follow Tim Gallwey's Inner Game instructions, which is to keep Self 2 out of the judgment process, and it usually works for around 35 seconds. Then I am likely to do all the things that "temperamental" players are prone to do. I call myself names. I grind my teeth. I pull my hair. I hit myself on the head with the racquet strings. I sulk.

No. 1 players, of course, do not engage in such childish behavior and so I can tell you that for two days last summer, I played tennis for about eight hours and never once called myself a name (except in jest, of course), never once ground my teeth or pulled my hair, never once hit myself on the head with the racquet strings, never once sulked.

The really amazing part, though, is that I started playing in those two days much better tennis than I normally play (or were the other players so intimidated, they were unable to put any pressure on?). My double fault vanished. I was volleying better (although, admittedly, what other players were calling "great drop volleys" were actually mis-hits), and I was playing with uncharacteristic consistency. "You mean you didn't start playing until you were past 30?"One man in his mid-40's exclaimed to me in all earnestness. "That's an inspiration to me. It really is."

Wow! What do you say when somebody tells you that you're an "inspiration"?

On my last night at Gray Rocks, they gave out the awards. For each of my tournament victories, I won a red and gold ribbon with a No. 1 written on it, together with a small pin. One of the ribbons is staring at me from my bulletin board, and it invariably draws a question from people who stop by and notice it. So far, about seven of my friends have asked about it and have been told what it represents: a tournament victory in Canada. They have all been impressed—all except for Walter. Walter is a frequent tennis partner of mine and, as it turns out, he went to Gray Rocks a year or two before I did, a fact I didn't realize until I got back and told him where I'd been.

"That's a real coincidence," Walter said, before he'd seen my ribbon. "Do they still have those tournaments up there?"

"They do, indeed," I said, and pointed to the bulletin board.

"That's amazing," Walter said.

"What's amazing?" I said, a little defensively maybe. "That I won the tournament?"

"No," Walter said. "I won the same tournament. I have the same red ribbon at home."

"You're kidding," I said.

"No," Walter insisted. "Although to tell you the truth, the competition wasn't all that great. Was it the same for you?"

"Sort of," I said.

"Who cares," Walter said. "A win is a win."

Indeed. So what if my opponents that week at Gray Rocks were not exactly Forest Hills material. So what if it was just a friendly little resort tournament .

The facts speak for themselves. Only a handful of people, I have since been told, have won both the mixed and men's doubles tournament at Gray Rocks and I am one of them.

"It's hell all right. Advanced players can only play against beginners."

ROOFTOP
TENNIS
CLUB

"Nice try, Farkus!"

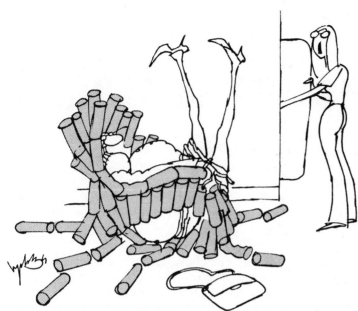

"Frank made that chair out of tennis ball cans..."

"I understand he's making a fortune on those group lessons of his..."

The Racquet as Scalpel

WILLIAM WALDEN

Although I have read many books of tennis instruction over the years, I cannot recall any that recommended hitting oneself with the racquet while playing. Tennis teachers whom I have queried about the practice are inclined, to a man, to disapprove of it, and very few players have a good word to say for it. As far as I have been able to determine, it is almost universally regarded as a gauche, amateurish act. Hardly anybody will admit to doing it deliberately, and those who do it accidentally adopt a shame-faced or facetious tone when it happens. If the blow should draw blood, they quickly slap on a Band-aid and apologize for having delayed the game.

It was therefore startling and, in a way, refreshing for me to encounter a tournament-calibre player with a quite different view on the subject. This man not only hits himself with a racquet occasionally but does so deliberately.

Joe, as I shall call him, frequently beats players of superior ability. He leans heavily on psychology in his game and, as might be expected, employs various stratagems intended to disconcert his opponent. In his repertory are such time-honored ones as overdeliberateness when changing courts or preparing to receive service, bouncing the ball eight or 10 times before serving it, tying his shoelaces or carefully examining his racquet strings after losing a hard-fought point that has winded him, looking incredulous when a close call goes against him, and glaring fiercely at a linesman to intimidate him.

But Joe by no means limits himself to hoary tricks. One of his less familiar ones is hitting himself with his racquet, which he says can offer enormous advantages if skillfully exploited. To provide maximum benefit, it must be used sparingly (certainly no more than once a match), at a critical juncture, and in a seemingly accidental manner.

He cites the following situation as an example: You are engaged in a hard-fought singles match where the sets are even and the games 4-all in the final one. You are serving, and it's ad out. If your opponent wins the next point and the game, he will probably serve out the match in the following game. According to Joe, this is a perfect time for the racquet-hitting gambit.

"You use an exaggerated twist on your first service, making sure the ball does not enter the service box and that on your downward swing the racquet hits your thigh just above the knee," Joe explains. "A metal racquet is best for the purpose because it cuts skin more easily, but you can achieve the same result with wood racquets if you work at it. Like any tennis stroke, it takes considerable practice to bring off properly, and by 'properly' I mean drawing blood, because without it the whole maneuver is wasted.

"Let's assume that on this occasion you are successful — you clip yourself smartly and begin to bleed. Time is called, and someone rushes onto the court to offer you a bandage. *Refuse it!* Resolutely wave away all offers of help. A little blood won't inconvenience you, and your refusal will accomplish the following: You prove yourself a true sportsman by not delaying the game in order to apply a bandage. You appear stoic and heroic. You gain the sympathy of the spectators; they will probably root for you to win, and that can be a big morale-booster. Most important, you also disturb your opponent. His concentration has been broken by the accident; the sight of your blood flowing may also make him jittery. It is not improbable that when play is resumed he will smash your second service into the net or over the fence.

"If he is made of sterner stuff and puts away your second service for a winner, you may have to resort to the more extreme measure of wiping your bleeding thigh on your shirt. This is not as difficult as it may sound. Simply bring up your knee smartly to various parts of your chest several times, to spread the gore around promiscuously. (Your shirt should be white or at the very least a pale color, to provide contrast. Red shirts—even pink ones—are definitely *out*.) Unless your opponent has nerves of steel, he is bound to find it harder to pass you at the net if you come charging up to it in a blood-spattered shirt. Your wound should achieve significant results for you, and it may even turn the tide. It has done so for me more than once. Of course, I resort to it only when I'm behind in important matches."

I asked Joe whether the same result could not be achieved by "accidentally" running into a net post while chasing a sharply angled shot, or by falling and twisting one's ankle slightly. He vetoed these as definitely inferior.

"You miss the point," he said to me. "A fall or a collision would elicit audience sympathy, but it might also hamper or even incapacitate you. You want to handicap your opponent, not yourself. Very few self-inflicted injuries accomplish this. Blood-drawing with a racquet is ideal, because it can nonplus your opponent without limiting your mobility."

Joe regards the lower thigh as the easiest place to hit oneself, but he does not restrict himself to that area. He sometimes clobbers himself on the opposite elbow, on the calf, or over the eyebrow. The calf cut is the least useful because, not being double-jointed, he cannot wipe the blood on his shirt or shorts, where it would be more conspicuous, but only on his other sock, and even that is often difficult. On the other hand, the cut over the eye, which is the most difficult to inflict, pays the greatest dividends. It makes him look like a prize-fighter who has been butted by his opponent, and he immediately becomes the sympathetic underdog. By some obscure sports-image-transference process that Joe does not pretend to understand, the audience assumes his opponent to have been guilty of foul play, and thereafter displays marked hostility toward him.

Joe capitalizes fully on the reaction. He hastily wipes the blood on his shirt, blinks several times as if to clear his clouded vision, and then, to the applause of the spectators, announces that he is ready to play. His demoralized opponent, who usually is not, either doublefaults, misjudges a bounce, or finds himself on the wrong foot when attempting a return. Shaken, he tries to gather himself together and steady himself, but the sight of his gore-smeared opponent unnerves him. In no time at all, his game hits the skids and slides quickly downhill until it becomes a shambles, permitting Joe to walk off with the match.

Joe· has many other tricks in his bag, but he is understandably chary about sharing them with me. He has promised, however, that one day he will write a book on how to play winning tennis that won't offer a single word of advice about covering the court, anticipating returns, or improving strokes. I look forward to reading it when it is published.

Man against Man, with Civility

**THEODORE
SOLOTAROFF**

First, some words to the unwary about the author of the following report on the competitive aspects of tennis. My credentials in this field are not striking, consisting mainly of the facts that I play tennis and have a competitive temperament (though this last point bristles with qualifications that will emerge as we go along). In any case, the larger reaches of the subject are closed to me: I have never played in a tennis tournament or belonged to a team, and I have no ranking whatsoever, not even on the "ladder" at the Central Park courts. My game isn't up to any of that. What you'll be getting, then, is a report from the lower depths of the tennis scene, where the paunchy, middle-aged, middle-range players contend, banging away at their opponents and themselves, looking to win back a little of what they are losing to the caricaturing hand of time and the world's slow stain.

I didn't take up tennis until I was in my mid-30's. Being reasonably adept at sports, I soon looked like a tennis player, but there was more form than content to my game. After I had been playing for a few months, a court veteran told me that I was either the worst good player he had ever seen or the best bad one, and advised me to take some lessons. But I was too eager to play matches to bother with instruction, even though I had played golf for a couple of years before a friend showed me how to hold the club properly, which immediately corrected a habitual slice and lengthened my drives by 50 yards. Live and unlearn.

Some 10 years and many frustrating hours later, my strokes are about as sound as they would have been if I had initially taken 20 lessons and my over-all game has progressed to somewhere around a B-minus: a swift first serve which Arthur Ashe himself told me (one of the fringe benefits of a sales conference) that he was going to leave alone; a strong if capricious forehand; and, when things are going well, a serviceable backhand. I still tend to be handcuffed at the net by a hard return and my overhead game is still for the birds. I am reasonably fast and agile, but short on endurance. In a tough singles match I fuss around as much between serves as Luis Tiant does between pitches. My poor wind keeps me in the backcourt as much as possible and prods me to hit for winners when I should be just keeping the ball in play. I also do a lot of lobbing. All of which works fairly well with most of my regular opponents, who have their own problems, but a steady player who moves me around the court will have me at his mercy within a set.

My main trouble, though, is not stamina but imagination. Like Henry James, I have the imagination of disaster, which works better for modern literature than it does for tennis. In general, imagination is the neurotic tennis player's substitute for concentration. Concentration means that you are following a clear-cut set of orders:

"Move to the ball, get your racquet back, set your feet, see the ball, squeeze the handle, stride, see the ball meet the racquet, follow through," and so forth. But my imagination can't be bothered with such mundane matters; it's usually too busy adjusting my play to the image I happen to have of myself at the moment. Thus, if I have hit a couple of backhand errors in a row, my imagination appears on the scene like a doctor in the house to announce that my backhand has suffered a relapse and my following strokes will be timid with dismay and caution. If I have just hit a forehand smash down the line in a close match and my opponent has somehow gotten it back, imagination raises the deadening question of what do I have to do to win a point. Or if I am coming in for a weak return, with three-fourths of the court sitting wide open, my imagination will turn grandiose and suggest a really decisive smash or a classy dropshot. This is also known as the death wish.

Imagination also provides the difference between those crisp, fluent strokes that I make while warming up and those tense, tentative ones when the game begins. With the first serve, I am no longer out for the exercise or to improve my skill; I am not even contending against the actual person on the other side of the net but rather against the familiar imagery and feelings of defeat. A shot that goes out by an inch or two is prophetic of all the other bad luck to come. A flubbed ground stroke at my ad means the loser in me is already out of the bag. And, of course, the more I want to win or, at least, perform well, the more acute this state of mind is.

To be sure, my imagination may sometimes turn rosy and breathe confidence and even panache into my game. If the other player is palpably more inconsistent than I am, I can turn into the clever court strategist with the big shot up his sleeve, and my strokes become surprisingly accurate. Or, playing against a woman, even one who is a tough opponent, a certain gallantry sets in that makes me relaxed and good-natured and smooths out my game. Or if I'm in a match with someone whose game and temperament complement and steady mine, I become the dogged competitor, hanging in there, taking the bad shots and breaks with the good ones, coolly dueling for the edge of confidence that will be decisive. Or I may find myself giving a good game for a while to a superior player, and then the years melt away and I am the talented newcomer on his way up. That's when the dazzling shots tend to come off my racquet. With nothing to lose I am free to hit out—impressiveness is all. I also tend to play better when I'm down three or four games or have lost a set. Then I can take on my oldest and probably favorite role — the gritty underdog, losing but not quitting, pulling himself up from the canvas like Wayne Morris in "Kid Galahad" and slowly, steadily fighting back, regaining his poise. On the other hand, let me get ahead 5-3 and 40-love in a tough match, and my right hand will lose its cunning as though I were the Psalmist forgetting Jerusalem.

Before I became a flashy, erratic tennis player, I

was a flashy, erratic golfer, and before that—back in high school and in the Navy—a flashy, erratic basketball player. So a certain continuity is clearly operating here, known as personality, which transcends the sharply differing demands of these three sports. *Ca m'est egal.* Golf was like writing fiction, a solitary activity in which one secretly competed with the masters and predictably fell short, but now and then produced an inspired stroke or two that matched the dream. Tennis, the sport I turned to, was more like writing criticism, the form I turned to after giving up fiction—a companionable activity that involved a relationship both supportive and competitive.

Unless you're one of those George Allens of the tennis courts—to whom winning isn't everything: it's the only thing—you try to form tennis relationships in which the competitive side and what might be called the "play" side are held in balance. In other words, the rivalry that adds zest and interest to the match does not get out of hand and take away the pleasure of the game itself, which includes the physical exertion, the enjoyment of your portion of talent and strength, the development of your skill, the satisfaction of well-played points and, in a taut close match, the manifold interest of the little drama in which you're participating. In short, you depend on your tennis buddy to give you a "good game"—with all that implies—without the aggressions spilling over. In general, tennis tends to foster a certain civility of competition. Indeed, it is part of the game's tradition and mystique. There is no athletic event that is more genteel than a major tennis tournament — the posh surroundings, the austere white uniforms (turning slightly mod these days), the practice of referring to the players as Mr., Mrs., or Miss, the extraordinary politeness of the fans who remain totally silent during play, discreetly clap to show their approval, and respond to a bad call by a gentle volley of whistling. This decorum tends to trickle down to the plebeian sectors of the tennis scene. You are not supposed to be noisy on the court or taunt your opponent. You also depend on your opponent for good sportsmanship, since he calls the shots on his side of the court. Where there isn't this trust, tennis becomes poisonous. And finally, in good singles and doubles a feeling of comity often develops between or among the players that is stronger than I have found in any other sport. For one thing, there is no direct physical contact to whip up tempers. For another, there is the back-and-forth movement of the ball that binds the two or four players together, so that a well-played point is something shared as well as won or lost.

Which is not to say that tennis doesn't arouse the blood feelings. Under the stress of a close match, it doesn't take much to set them off—a few questionable calls, a certain cockiness in your opponent, a lucky shot or two on his part and a few near-misses on yours. But unlike the contact sports, there is not much you can do with hostility on a tennis court, which is one reason why the sport is as much an emotional workout as it is a physical one. Just as your strokes require careful control, so does your head. Too much aggression and you lose your touch, too little and you lose your competitive edge. I guess this is why tennis makes you talk to yourself so much; beneath that relatively impassive decorum flows a stream of abuse and self-abuse, of oaths and imprecations, of gloating and encouragement by which the mind struggles to clear itself and function, to mobilize muscle and sinew and to strike some degree of balance between combativeness and cool.

Perhaps it's the encroaching sedateness of middle age that makes me tend to confine my tennis these days to people I like to play with and where the aggressions are monitored by long-standing relationships. This hasn't always been the case. There was a time when I played a lot at the courts in Central Park and went in for pick-up matches with the regulars there. Many of them were older men, often refugees, or so I imagined, with one or another of the Central European accents. They were typically small, stocky, ungraceful men, with herky-jerky little serves and soft, wily groundstrokes, and they had a particular talent for keeping the ball in play and you at loose ends, a process that would begin on the porch of the clubhouse.

"Care to play some singles?" I would ask casually.

The silence of a man mulling over a dubious proposition. He would be sitting there in his clean whites and shower clogs, having already played once that afternoon and now relaxing after his shower—a person of means fallen to the level of a public tennis club but making do. I imagined that this group all made their living by intricate financial dealings in the morning which left the rest of the day free for tennis. He might finally reply, "And how is your game?"

"Not bad. I can probably give you a pretty good match."

"You sink so, young man" — slowly nodding his head, pursing his lips, still doubtful. "And how long have you been playing tennis?"

"Oh, four or five years. I'm really not bad."

And so we sign up, my friend using one of his three permits which, along with some judicious tips, enable him to play as much as he likes even when there is a four-hour wait for a court. He changes into his tennis shoes and I follow him out to our court. "Your balls are satisfactory?" he asks quickly, which settles that issue. He places his towel over the end of the net cord just so, slips on his elbow brace like a gauntlet, and strides off. In the warm-up he shows very little besides his methodicalness: "More to ze backhand, please." He is also a little slow about going up to the net to retrieve the balls that have been hit there. His shots come across the net nice and easy, and I smash a few crosscourt forehands, feeling my oats and to let him know what's what. He watches them go by with a disdainful little shrug. Then he hits a few balls that are heavy with topspin and announces he is ready.

After only a few points, it is clear that he knows my weaknesses better than I do. He attacks my backhand until he gets an error or a weak return that he skips in and puts away. He lures me into the middle of the court and then hits past me into the corners. If I rush the net, he chips down the sideline or lobs flatly over my head. If I hang back, he hits his cunning little drop shots. His different spins, particularly on the lumpy, rutted clay of the Central Park courts, are murder. My first serve isn't going in, my forehand is either too cautious or too reckless, my backhand has all but collapsed and I feel as if my pants are down around my ankles. There is no quarter coming from the other side of the court; instead, there are his little struts, shrugs and grunts of self-satisfaction, and the disdainful sweep of his hand to indicate that still another of my shots has gone out.

It usually took a set or so before I could begin to get into the match. First, the dues had to be paid to my nervousness, then the venting of my anger at this conceited demon who was toying with me, then the apathy that followed of believing that nothing would work, that I was simply outclassed. The next stage would be the coming to my senses, usually by way of seeing the comedy I had gotten myself into. "It's only a game," I would say drolly to myself. And soon my first serve would start going in. I would begin to get my racquet back and to look at the ball, and the other side of the court would grow bigger and less protected. Also my smug friend across the net would begin to make some errors. As the match tightened up, its mood would become less oppressive. By the end, we would be complimenting each other.

There's a moral in all this which my tennis career, such as it is, has demonstrated over and over again but which I've been slow to grasp and accept. Namely, that competitiveness isn't good for me. Or, to put it more bluntly, I'm not a good competitor, not in tennis or any other sport.

It's a hard thing for an American, particularly a former jock, to admit. But it's not as hard as it used to be. Many of us are beginning to wise up to the truth that winning isn't the only thing, nor is losing the worst—a truth whose force we witnessed in the course of the Watergate hearings and in reading the Pentagon Papers.

No, competition doesn't necessarily bring out the best in you. And the better part of the consciousness of the young people whose major sport became Frisbee is that competitiveness has been driving many of us in America a bit crazy. Before we could lay waste most of

Southeast Asia, we first had to have all those winners in Washington enamored of the mentality of professional football, a populace that prided itself on being unde-featable, and a society in which competition is the name of the game. "We are here as winners, not losers," President Nixon once announced to his fellow Repub-licans as he stood at bay. It does give one pause.

It takes a lot of deconditioning for a middle-class American Jew (a whole other subject) like me to con-trol, much less give up, his competitive instincts, and I can't say that I have made more than a dent. But a tennis court is a good place to begin. If I get far enough, I may even take up golf again—just for the fun of it.

"I thought this meatball tasted strange. It's been approved by the USTA."

NEW MIRACLE TENNIS METHOD INSTANTLY HELPS YOUR GAME

"There are at least a dozen patients ahead of you . . . but I think he'll see you right this minute."

"Play two."

"They never let you forget, do they?"

It Only Hurts When I Serve

MARLENE FANTA SHYER

I used to think that tennis elbow was nothing more than a sore arm, but now I know the difference. A sore arm is to tennis elbow what a sneeze is to double pneumonia, what a sparrow is to a pterodactyl, what a parking ticket is to being chained to the wall of a dungeon for seven years. Tennis elbow means you can't turn on your car's ignition key, spray your hair, lift your glass of gin-and-tonic or spank your kids.

Worst of all, you can't play tennis. And for tennis freaks like me (albeit third-rate tennis freaks), giving up fun at the courts is not much better than being chained up for seven years.

It is true that tennis elbow afflicts people whose occupations also put stress on the common extensor tendon—like construction workers, dental surgeons and hatchet murderers. But my tennis elbow came from a crazy backhand and a serve that looks like I'm hanging laundry.

One day, I had the same old sore arm I've lived with for the seven years I've been playing tennis. I ignored it through three sets as usual, and the next morning—zing—last year's Bicentennial took on a new meaning: I saw stars and stripes when I tried to pick up my toothbrush to brush my teeth and saw the rockets' red glare when I dialed the number of our neighborhood orthopedist.

The orthopedist has a reputation for having a way with tennis injuries; also a heart of gold. He sympathetically recommended putting ice on the point of injury at every opportunity, no exercising of the arm, switching to a steel racquet and a cortisone shot. The cortisone shot was heaven. In went the needle and out went the pain. I shook his hand gratefully and without screaming; indeed, he did have a heart of gold!

Unfortunately, it turned out he had a bank account to match—a topseeded bill arrived at about the same time the pain recurred.

"No problem," said the doctor. "Come down for a second shot. Safe, these shots are really safe."

"How come you don't give more than three, then?" I asked, as I dubiously rolled up my sleeve. I have a fear of things that could be banned by the FDA for giving you bald spots, I have a fear of the stuff used to treat bald spots and I am also afraid of black bats.

"I've given up to four of these shots. Once I gave five."

"Why five? Why not six? What would happen to me if I had six shots? Would I lose my hair? My life? Would I begin to see black bats?"

"Try not to play for two weeks," said the doctor. "You'll be fine!"

Two weeks later, feeling fine, I jumped into my white dress, white sneakers and matching three-inch surgical elbow-band and rushed to the courts for my game. I played as well as I can play and, as I remember, won. That night, with a teardrop springing out of each eye, I searched our medicine cabinet for morphine. "Why me?" I spoke to the pinched, tennis-white face in the mirror. "Why not Billie Jean or Evonne or Martina or one of those court-hogs? I only want to play an hour and a half a day! Am I asking too much of the tennis gods?"

I began to hear a great deal about a famous big-city bone doctor, Dr. Supreme—the medical divinity of all injured jocks—who might be able to help me. By pulling every conceivable string, I was able to get an appointment with Dr. Supreme three months hence, unless there was an earlier cancellation. Three months passed without a cancellation (clearly nobody would *think* of canceling an appointment with Dr. Supreme) and my day came.

Down to the city I flew, arriving neurotically early so as to be certain that I did not keep Dr. Supreme waiting so much as a minute; into the waiting room I rushed, greeted by enough other waiters to warrant hot dog vendors and a Good Humor truck; fortunately

I was able to find a seat, a magazine and a good view of the smiling football and baseball greats whose autographed faces looked down from the walls. The receptionist called my name an hour and 40 minutes later without a trace of guilt in her voice.

Into the great doctor's office I went, hushed, suppliant. I had just heard his great voice on the radio last week, being interviewed again. Here he was in the flesh, diamond glittering on his finger, boredom glittering in his eyes. He read my medical history (filled into appropriate mimeo'd blanks in the waiting room), dropped a few famous tennis names he'd (very successfully) treated, told me to apply wet heat to the point of injury at every opportunity, to exercise with rubber bands and never to take cortisone shots because they were very bad for me.

Dr. Supreme also told me that people more than age 50 and people under 30 were hardly ever afflicted, which wasn't much consolation for someone who was missing immunity by 10 years in any direction. Then he massaged my elbow until my protests reached high C; an "ancient method of therapy" he explained and, yawning again, he made it clear that he had better things to do than examine suburban matrons with tennis elbows.

Dr. Supreme's ancient method of therapy set my arm so far back that I had to press the elevator button with my left hand and ask the cleaning lady to open my bottle of asprin when Dr. Supreme's statement came. I hadn't been near a tennis court in more than three months and it still felt as if electric barbed wires were short-circuiting in my arm. If medical science was not going to help me, where then was I to turn?

To Dr. Foo, who had treated any number of tennis elbows successfully with acupuncture, and who would see me only if I had a special introduction from a friend (preferably not a friend who was a detective and would lock her up for practicing without a needle license). Dr. Foo is located in a high-rise in the part of the city into which it is best to venture only with a friend at each side—preferably off-duty killers.

No bowing mandarin greeted me at Dr. Foo's apartment door. Little Dr. Foo herself, wearing T-shirt and blue jeans, ushered me into her foyer, past her living room, her kitchen, to her examining room. Here was a spartan examining table, a desk with a drawer in it for money, a chair and a peanut butter jar filled with long, thin needles. These she stuck into my arm here and there, giving each a jaunty little twirl, letting them stand at attention in my skin like toothpicks in hors d'oeuvres for a minute or two and then, pulling them out.

While I screamed my little screams, Dr. Foo assured me that I would be praying tennis velly soon. I wanted to believe her. "Are you a medical doctor, Dr. Foo?" I asked hopefully, looking in vain for a diploma on the walls. "Herbal doctor," she said, and my blood ran cold. Could one sue an herbal doctor for malpractice if a needle slipped into the wrong pore and gave one bald spots?

Then I thought that maybe the reason I had tennis elbow in the first place was just that there was no peanut butter in my bloodstream. One of my health-food aficionado friends assured me that if I was eating the right supplements, I'd have gotten rid of my pain long ago.

The proprietor of the health food store concurred. He laid it on me organically: vitamin B6, calcium, vitamin C. "Does this really work for tennis elbow?" I asked, skeptical as ever.

"We have never had a failure!" he said with such authority one had to believe him, even as he called me back as I was leaving the store. "You know, of course, that this can't work if you eat citrus fruit?"

"No citrus fruit? Not even orange juice for breakfast?"

His eyes rolled up in his head. "You've been drinking orange juice? Oh, my God! No wonder you have tennis elbow!"

So there it was! Orange juice had given me tennis elbow! The Forest Hills and Wimbledon gang clearly had known it all along, but they weren't telling *me*. It took the healthfood store man to let me in on the big secret. I wanted to believe. I quit orange juice, grapefruits and lemon in my tea. No more citrus fruits for enlightened me. I took vitamins morning, noon and night—and I felt the health just mobilize in every part of me.

Except my elbow, which was as bad as ever.

But wait! Why not chiropractic? A lady down the street, formerly sciatic and now able to dance the Hustle, et al, recommended Dr. Spinelly, who was equipped with all the latest therapy machines.

His waiting room was decorated by a life-sized stainless steel backbone illuminated by indirect lighting and an old group photo of a graduating class of the New York Chiropractic Institute. Had I chosen the right graduate? If I hadn't, would I be leaving here via ambulance, or worse, under a sheet covering my bald spots, broken body, et al? I was reassured by the positive reading material in the waiting room, read the testimonials of the celebrities who, with their pain-free arms, applaud chiropractic: Joan Crawford, Robert Goulet, Marlo Thomas and Norma Zimmer. *Norma Zimmer?*

Dr. Spinelly reassured me, too. He talked about kinesiology and the integrated nervous system. He drew diagrams on a blackboard in his book-lined office.

Then, off to the manipulating table, where I lay comfortably prone while Dr. Spinelly did his push-pull, click-click bit. He never touched my elbow at all. He pressed and squeezed here and there between neck and hips as if he were demonstrating the kneading of yeast buns. I got up from the table feeling light-headed but pretty good, ready for the next step in therapy— the ionic pulse machine. Dr. Spinelly rolled the gorilla-sized grey box over to my chair, directed its conical nozzle toward my liver.

"Why the liver?" I asked.

"Didn't I explain about the integrated nervous system?" Dr. Spinelly asked, as he good-naturedly pulled out an illustrated volume showing the connection between tennis elbow and the liver. Then he turned on the machine. It went "Rrrr" and a red light blinked on. Dr. Spinelly set the timer and left me under the watchful eye of the red light. "Rrrr."

When the timer went "ding" 20 minutes later, Dr. Spinelly was back rolling yet another behemoth in my direction. "Ultrasound therapy," he said.

"Won't hurt, trust me," said Dr. Spinelly, and he began rubbing white cream on my arm in a circular motion. Next, he set the dial, turned on a switch and the machine activated. "Zmzmzmz." He massaged my creamed arm with an attachment not unlike a mini floor waxer. "Zmzmzmzm." For all its Isaac Asimov overtones, the whole treatment was one big party.

Unfortunately, a friend then brought me the copy of the consumer's guide magazine which featured a long evaluation of chiropractic therapy. As I turned the pages (ouch, ouch, ouch) I resigned myself sadly to a new philosophy: where there is life there is hope, but where there is an Achilles heel of the elbow, one must take up kickball—or wait for the great orthopedist-in-the-sky to do His thing.

Wait!

Word has just reached me about an incredible drug called DMSO. When applied topically, it miraculously banishes all elbow pain and furthermore, as a nifty dividend, also improves intelligence. Unfortunately, DMSO is banned here by the FDA and is available only in parts of Russia or at your local veterinarian's. That might explain why Russians are smart and why dogs are free of tennis elbow. But it leaves the rest of us with our white dresses yellowing in our closets, too dumb and in too much pain to lift the telephone book to look up faith healers in the yellow pages.

Unless!

Does Blue Shield, by any chance, cover voodoo?

A Few Frissons at Forest Hills

**LAURENCE
SHEEHAN**

I always enjoyed the tennis action out at Forest Hills, whether it was any good or not, because it's so much trouble getting out there that I'll be damned if I don't have a nice time.

One year when the Open was still played there I lucked into tickets for good seats for Saturday—the usually eventful day of the men's semifinals and the women's final—so I didn't mind putting up with the trucks on the Connecticut Turnpike, the tie-ups at the tolls for the Whitestone Bridge, and finally the frenzy of Queens Boulevard, a six- or eight-lane concourse, depending on whether the cars are using the sidewalks on that particular day.

I didn't even mind getting lost after I turned off Queens Boulevard and parked in the maze of shaded one-way streets in the vicinity of the tournament site. Unlike most great sports centers—the Coliseums of Rome and New Haven, for example—the West Side Tennis Club does not stand apart from its surroundings, but is buried in them somewhere. After you've parked your car a couple of miles from the place, having turned left and right at random a dozen times in search of a slot, you haven't the foggiest idea where you are. I usually solve this problem by tagging along behind other arriving tennis fans who look as if they can tell north from south. But this day I followed a family group (in retrospect, they were too well dressed for a tennis tournament) and they led me to a synagogue in the opposite direction from the club. It was the first day of the Jewish New Year and they were going there to worship.

Anyway, I backtracked and finally found the club and got to my seat only a few minutes late for the day's opening semifinal match between defending Open champion Jimmy Connors and the young Swedish player Bjorn Borg (pronounced *yong swee-dish play-er b'yorn borg*).

There were two points that made me jump to my feet in this particular match between two of the greatest tennis players in the world. The first was in the first set when the Goodyear blimp seemed to be going out of control in the swirly winds high above the stadium. It tilted back some 45 degrees and wobbled dangerously from side to side before righting itself and resuming its vital role as Peeping Tom to all of America's major televised sports events.

The second was when Billie Jean King walked in behind my row at the start of the third set and took a seat three boxes away. At the very next change of sides on the court I stood up to stretch and to review the BJK phenomenon. I decided she looked great in her new "natural" hairdo and her tweedy slacks outfit and that Penguin paperback under the arm. In a little while she would be watching the match between Chris Evert and Evonne Goolagong to decide the women's singles championship. If memory served, it would be the first time that Billie Jean King, as a major figure in competition, had not gone after one of the big women's singles titles. This historic moment of withdrawal, if not outright retirement, did not seem to weigh heavily on Ms. King, however. The promoter of various feminist causes in and out of sports chatted amiably with the folks around her and seemed to be in great spirits, as happy as—I was going to say as happy as a girl . . .

Actually, there were many points that held my attention during the three-hour-long match which Connors won over Borg 7-5, 7-5, 7-5. But I never jumped to my feet for the type of tennis played because there were no dramatic shifts in fortune, or changes in tactics, to give excitement to the match.

Connors held and kept a slight edge throughout. Borg had his only good chance to change things when Connors was down two break points serving at 5-5 in the second set. If Borg had broken that serve and then gone on to win his own serve, the match would have been all even, one set apiece, and we might have been able to watch them rally for five hours instead of three.

Matches that become both routine and long give you time to take your eye off the ball and to concentrate on comparing the playing styles and on-court personalities of the players out there, especially if you are blessed with seats close enough to the action to be able to discern the S.A.S. (for Scandinavian Airlines, I bet) on Bjorn's shoulder, or the gold bauble around Jimmy's neck, and thus have something trivial and therefore significant to base your contrast on.

Borg's a right-hander who likes to stay back at the baseline and hit topspin passing shots or topspin lobs for winners. Connors is a leftie who can stay back or come up to the net with equal skill, though on the slow clay surface which has replaced the grass for the matches at Forest Hills, he usually stayed back, too.

The two players' groundstrokes *sound* different. Borg's racquet has a "B" designed into the color pattern of its strings, which seems to signify not so much the name of the racquet's manufacturer as the tinny *boing* noise that Borg creates when he imparts extreme topspin to balls, producing shots that clear the net in a looping trajectory and then fall sharply and usually a bit short on the other side.

Connors' racquet has a "W" written into the strings which, if only Wilson Sporting Goods did not object, could be said to stand for the *whomp* you hear whenever Connors hits the ball—his long, flat stroking action producing square and low-flying shots of great depth.

The two players also have quite different ways about them on court. Borg is silent when he hits the ball, and Connors grunts at every exertion. Borg is expressionless to the point of seeming to brood—has he watched too many Bergman movies in his native Sweden? Connors is animated and always on the lookout for a chance to be melodramatic or clownish — too many John Wayne movies and Bob Hope shows, clearly.

But enough of this idle speculation. The new clay

court surface was the talk of Forest Hills, not any particular player or match-up.

This was the first year the U.S. Championships were played on clay rather than on grass. In recent years the pros had argued more and more vociferously that the grass courts at Forest Hills deteriorated too rapidly under tournament conditions to provide a fair test. Too many bad bounces by the time the quarter-finals rolled around, said the pros.

Anyway, after the 1974 Open the turf was ripped up from the stadium and from a dozen field courts. It was replaced by sacks and sacks of Har-Tru, a gray, ground-up greenstone surface which I happen to be familiar with from my indoor doubles game on Monday nights during the winter. Quite early in the Connors-Borg match, I realized there were various things I can do on Har-Tru that the pros have not yet mastered—such as standing flatfooted, running in place, and tripping over the sideline on return of serve.

Nevertheless, there are a couple of good things about the switch to clay at Forest Hills. For one, the red geraniums encircling the stadium grounds coordinate better with the gray of the Har-Tru than they did with the green of the real grass. For another, the new setup locates one clay court in the middle of the playing area and thus centralizes the focus of the event. Under the old setup there were *two* grass courts in the stadium on which play alternated, and that always left half the fans farther away from the action than they felt they deserved to be. Furthermore, with only one court in the stadium, more space has materialized for installing high-priced box seats. That spells more bucks for the sponsoring U.S. Lawn Tennis Association, and so more money to hire officials who can refuse press credentials to writers like myself who find themselves temporarily out of work or—worse, in the eyes of the USLTA—on assignment for newspapers or magazines with circulations under 400 million.

As to the quality of the play itself, and without meaning to detract from the achievement of Evert in defeating Goolagong for the women's singles title

three hours after Connors beat Borg, or the achievement of the great slow-court player Manuel Orantes of
Spain in defeating Connors for the men's singles title
on the next day, I would have to say that, from a fan's
point of view, the winning tennis at Forest Hills this
year was kind of blah. The only time during the Connors-Borg match I experienced those little *frissons* of
pleasure that tend to fulfill the typical tennis viewer's
expectations was when Connors managed to get in
close to the net and hit swinging volleys for winners.
The secret in the appeal to fans like myself of such
things as the service ace, the winning volley, and the
powerful overhead or smash is in the way time is al-
tered—one might say stolen—by the successful execution of these particular shots. On slower surfaces like
Har-Tru there are too few opportunities for speed and
daring. From a modern fan's point of view the ideal
tennis surface is one that challenges good players to hit
almost as many balls in the air as they hit off the
bounce. Har-Tru, though I swear by it all winter long,
is not that surface.

Speaking of fans, I forgot to mention the capacity
crowd of 15,000 in the stadium that day. Carefully
assessing the athletic abilities of this mob at one point, I
decided that I would probably be seeded 9,500th if we
all got up and organized a tennis tournament among
ourselves, and made the 100-odd pros in the Open wait
for our autographs, and pay seventy-five cents for
every lukewarm hot dog one needed to eat to survive
through the next match, and $1.25 for jugs of Sangria
smaller than baby bottles.

Anyway, these fans handled themselves well in the
face of such grueling tennis, high prices, and the mile-
long rest-room lines. I had heard that a kind of rough
subway crowd had been out to the matches earlier in
the week and had taken their shirts off, and sweated
profusely, and hoarsely guffawed, and in general acted
like your typical Mets fan, not your typical tennis fan.
But I was pleased to note the dignity of the fans out
there on Saturday.

The quality of tennis fan was typified for me by the

way bad line calls were received by the crowd. You are not supposed to whistle at a bad line call in the piercing manner your old man used to call you home for supper. Rather, you are supposed to make an "O" with your lips and produce a soft, monotonous kind of whistle, a sound with the mild insistence of the *hoo-hoo* sound that Frenchmen make whenever they spot one of their government leaders on the street. Nice, but not nice. I heard that stylish sound on numerous occasions out at Forest Hills that Saturday; it's one big reason I was glad to be there.

"The first thing you've got to do is forget everything your husband ever told you."

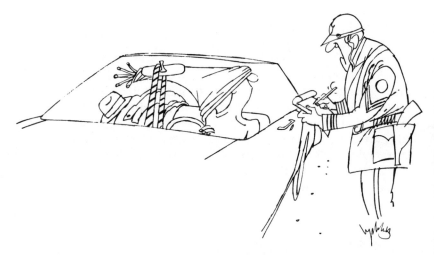

"You go right to the tennis court after work and it saves time if you dress in the car, uh, huh..."

"And my 4 a.m. Sunday morning starting time at the Lobber's Tennis Club I bequeath to my nephew and his wife."

"Here comes your first-round opponent. Now don't let him psych you out!"

"For heaven's sakes, Walter believe me—it was out!"

How to Ditch Your Doubles Partner Gracefully

BARRY TARSHIS

Even in the most idyllic of tennis relationships, there occasionally comes a time when one of the players wants to—well, call it quits. No tennis book or tennis article I've ever seen has looked into the question of how you engineer this uncomfortable business in a graceful way and, as far as I know, Tim Gallwey has no plans to write a book entitled "The Inner Game of Ditching." I figure it's time to give the matter some long overdue consideraion.

First of all, let's talk a little about how you can keep a separation amicable and prevent it from getting to a point where everybody ends up despising everybody else. There's only one way, really. It's up to the person about to be ditched (hereinafter referred to as the ditchee) to get wind of what's about to happen and, like a prudent executive on the way down, to jump before he's pushed.

Most of the time you become the ditchee when the player (or players) you've been playing with decide that you are no longer good enough to cut the mustard in his (or their) league. The problem, however, is that you yourself may not be aware—or may not be willing to acknowledge—that a cleavage has developed between your playing levels. Once at La Costa in California, for instance, I thought I was being as noble as Albert Schweitzer when I asked a player I'd just finished playing and considered a turkey among turkeys if he'd like to play again. "I don't want to hurt your feelings," he told me. "But I'm looking for a stronger game."

So he was. And so are most players, the theory

being that the only way to get better at tennis is to play with better players. But when it comes to a ditching situation, the question isn't who is, in fact, a better player but who *thinks* he's a better player. And so, if you want to avoid the prospect of being ditched, it's up to you to be sensitive to signs in the other player (or players) that he is contemplating a ditching move.

These signs are not difficult to discern. The first thing that usually happens when a tennis relationship is about to go on the rocks is that one partner is suddenly no longer as available for tennis dates as he used to be. You call to verify the tennis date that the two of you have kept on a weekly basis for the past 11 years and you are told something like: "Tomorrow, huh? Well, gee . . . let me see now. Tomorrow is such a crazy day. I have to go to the dentist and have six wisdom teeth pulled, and I may be getting my appendix taken out, and I have to see my lawyer about this $1 million lawsuit, and then I'm going to St. Louis. But if I see my way clear, I'll call you. O.K.?"

There are also changes in attitude on the court. All of a sudden you find that *you're* the one who's always bringing the balls. And if you suggest that there is a possible degree of inequity in the fact that you paid for the balls the last 12 times you've played, he's liable to tell you: "Look, if you're not happy with the way things are, why don't you find another partner?"

Much the same thing happens in a doubles relationship—particularly when three of the players come to the collective conclusion that the fourth player must be sacrificed. Having once been in this situation, I can tell you that there are more salubrious things for your ego than to be dumped from a tennis foursome. The best way to avoid an uncomfortable scene is to be sensitive to what's going on and make your exit as a dignified free agent and not as a downtrodden reject.

Beware the signs. You know you're in trouble when the other three players become overly solicitous (an indication that they are trying to salvage the situation by improving your confidence). Every time you miss a shot, they will say things like, "nice idea" or "good try." When you do happen to make a winning shot, they will react as if you've just returned from a moon walk. Eventually, alas, the support dissolves into a tight-lipped reticence. In my own situation, I began to suspect I was on the way out when sides were determined by one of the other three players saying, "O.K., I'll take Barry this time."

My advice if you find yourself in a similar situation is to cash in while you're ahead. If you start to ask questions about *next* season's arrangement, the chances are you are going to get answers more evasive than those received by the Watergate Committee. Executives who've never traveled in their lives will begin talking about a work schedule next year that will take them to more countries than Henry Kissinger has ever visited. Women will stress the importance of being "home more for the children," even though the kids are married and living in another part of the world. I'm not condemning the practice of making excuses, mind you. On the contrary, it's a much more civilized way of saying that you're not really wanted than to come out and flatly say that you're really not wanted.

I know some people who have tried to fight against being ditched but I don't recommend it. Tears won't work—certainly not in a men's game. Threats will only be taken seriously if you are well connected with the Mafia and, even then, may not do the job.

So as you can see, you don't have too many options as a ditchee. Once a tennis player doesn't want to play with you anymore, there isn't a great deal you can do to change his mind. The best you can do is to hope that sometime in the future — once your own game has undergone an improvement—you will run across a ditcher from your past in a local tournament of some kind. Should you whip him pretty good, you will have experienced one of the supreme joys in life. And this pleasure will be compounded when the player suggests that the two of you might possibly resume your playing arrangement. Since you've heard it all before, you'll know exactly what to say.

So much for the ditchee. In some respects, it's harder to be the person looking to escape a tennis relationship than it is to be somebody trying to hold one together. That's especially true if you are the sort of person who goes into convulsions anytime you step on an ant, and also true if the ditchee is somebody you have to deal with on a day-in and day-out basis—like your wife or husband, or boss.

I wish that I could recommend a specific strategy for ditching that is guaranteed to work without prompting the victim to seek retribution in the form of a contract for your execution. But I don't think I can.

You can be as evasive or as vague as you want to for a while, but if you're dealing with a ditchee who is not getting the message, sooner or later you're going to have to level with him. Fortunately, in a doubles situation, you can generally find somebody in your group who is good at this sort of thing. A hatchet man, in other words.

You shouldn't have trouble identifying the hatchet man in your foursome. His (or her) favorite stroke will be the overhead—a shot he'll try to hit even on low bouncing balls at the baseline. His favorite statesman will be Idi Amin. His favorite sports team will be the Philadelphia Flyers. He will favor a gun control referendum but only after all the pacifists in the United States have been shot. You will not have to beg him to break the news to the ditchee. He will volunteer. "Somebody has to do it," he'll say, trying his best to conceal a smile.

In the event none of the players in your group qualifies as a hatchet man, you will have to figure out some other way to select a player to do the deed. A telegram is a possibility but not a good one in my judgment. Too stagey—particularly if it's a singing telegram. The same for a note left in the locker. What's liable to happen when the ditchee gets the note is that he'll figure it's a joke. "You know what somebody left in my locker today?" he'll tell you, and you'll be right back where you started.

No, somebody has to take the responsibility: the person who's "organizing the game for next season." To determine who gets the job, you can draw straws, flip coins—maybe even stage a small tournament (talk about pressure!). In any case, make sure that the person who inherits the job won't turn around and blame everybody else in the group for the decision. ("Listen, Phil. I fought for you. Really, I did. But the other guys, they were impossible—especially Barry.")

And should you yourself be the unfortunate designee, I offer the following advice from one of the most accomplished hatchet men I know. "I don't make a big deal about it," he says, "When the guy comes up to me to ask about next year's game, I tell him we've already got the four players. Usually, he gets the message. If he doesn't and keeps asking questions like why and stuff like that, I figure he's asking for it, and so I tell him the truth—that the guys just don't enjoy playing with him."

Maybe it sounds a little harsh, but there are crueler ways of handling the situation. Ask Idi Amin.

"Put the leash away, boy, we're not going outside."

Net Loss

**RUSSELL
BAKER**

I put on my old sneakers and went to play tennis. I hated the idea, but there was no escape. All my friends played tennis. When they weren't playing tennis themselves, they watched other people playing tennis on television. In their leisure, they read books about tennis, and at night they went to each other's houses and talked about their backhands. Young couples in our circle were refusing to have babies and starting to have tennis racquets.

What could a man do? I put on my old sneakers and went to the courts. Everyone was scandalized. A friend hustled me away to avert a nasty incident. "Where did you get those shoes?" he asked.

They were black high-top sneakers I had worn in 1938 for playing softball at Carroll Park in South Baltimore. I hate to throw anything away, and they had served me well in many tight moments at shortstop.

"You can't go on the court wearing 38-year-old, black, high-top sneakers," he said.

I gathered that a tennis ball becomes so depressed upon seeing that it is being used by improperly dressed persons that it refuses to let itself be hit across the net. My black sneakers were not the only error in my haberdashery. The black nylon socks underneath them were offensive to all tenniskind, as were the purple corduroy slacks and torn Hawaiian shirt in which I had presumed to step on the court.

The discovery that tennis was not just a game, but also a boon for the clothing industry, was my first lesson. One needed $39 shoes, new socks and white suits that look like underwear for tycoons. I bought, and returned to the courts.

Friends folded double in laughter this time. "Where'd you get that racquet?" they asked. I had found it in the attic of a house we had bought in 1957.

The fact that it was made of wood and had a few gaps where there should have been strings struck everyone as hilarious. How did I expect ever to give Arthur Ashe a decent game with a racquet like that?

This was too much. While the racquet obviously wasn't the best, neither was I. In fact, the two of us seemed well suited. Big Bill Tilden, I argued, could have taken this very racquet and crushed Arthur Ashe, whereas I could play with the finest racquet ever made and not score a point against Arthur Ashe swinging a Ping-Pong paddle.

It was a losing argument. Friends pointed out that tennis isn't just a game and a boom for the clothing industry, but also a multimillion dollar bonanza for the sportsgoods business. For weeks these friends flooded me with conflicting advice about the greatest of all possible racquets for my particular game, which at that time was still no game at all because of the absence of the ideal racquet.

It finally boiled down to either a metal racquet or a handcrafted wooden racquet made only by an arthritic gnome who lived in the Italian Alps and refused to sell his miraculous works unless you went for an interview.

Friends urged me to buy one of each, pointing out that Jimmy Connors wouldn't dream of setting foot in Wimbledon with only one racquet. I could see that tennis was a thing of many racquets.

At last I was ready to play. With a new wardrobe, a fortune in racquets and a doctor's certificate pronouncing me fit for light exercise, I strode to the court and started to remove the wooden press from my first racquet. My friends dropped jaws and raised eyebrows. "You're still using a wooden press!" cried one.

"The new metal press is the only thing you should ever let touch your racquet," counseled another.

"Nonsense," said the third. "There is nothing better for a racquet than a fine wooden press, but"—here he turned to me—"this Korean ginkgo wood your press is made of should never be allowed in the same house with a decent racquet."

They began arguing seriously about metal versus wood. Somebody went home and got a tennis magazine which supported metal. Somebody else dashed off and came back with the latest book containing advice from Billie Jean King about wood. After an hour a thunderhead opened and the argument was rained out.

We actually played the next day. I hit the ball four times. Each time it went on to the adjoining court where a madman became infuriated because it kept distracting him from attaining the apoplectic seizure he was trying to achieve by losing to his wife. My friends were embarrassed and took me home. They tell me I had better not try playing until I have had a course of 16 lessons and spent a winter practicing every day at a Manhattan tennis club, which will only cost $3,600.

In the middle of writing all this, I stopped and put on my old black, high-top sneakers. Very comfortable. They may have cost $2.49 in 1938. They take me back to a time when games didn't lead inexorably to high blood pressure.

"How about a little something just to make the game interesting?"

The Tiddling Tennis Theorem

**ARTHUR
HOPPE**

The Tiddling Tennis Theorem, which in the end was to alter so drastically the lives of its advocates, was the product of a peculiar mind, that of John Doe Roberts. Roberts, who was never addressed by any name other than "Professor," had been the teaching professional at the Tiddling Tennis Club for as long as the oldest members could recall. The oldest, Doc Pritchgart, claimed the Professor, then a callow youth, had simply appeared one day following World War II when the club's membership had dwindled to 124 and had begun offering free tennis lessons. But as Doc Pritchgart was invariably more than $100 behind on his bar bill, invariably cheated at dominoes, and invariably denigrated the Professor whom he loathed with an unquenchable loathing, few trusted either his judgment, his recollection, or his veracity.

In any event, the Professor, now in his forties, could be found daily, barring rain, standing by the net of the teaching court, lecturing some aspirant to tennis immortality. He always wore the same yellowing flannel trousers, the same faded windbreaker, the same drooping Panama hat that shaded his thin, weathered features and surprisingly bright, deep-set brown eyes, and the same (Doc Pritchgart contended) unlit cigar between his large, clenched teeth.

"Let us turn to the techniques. How do you avoid an invitation from an inferior player? This depends solely on how inferior he is. If he is only slightly inferior and you may wish to play with him if no one better wanders in, the proper response is: 'Thank you. I'd love to play, but I think I already have a game, I think.' The advantage of hedging is that as the morning wanes and you grow increasingly desperate, you can approach him with the happy news that the game you said you thought you had has failed to materialize, thank God, because you would much rather play with him. No harm done. But if the invitation is extended by a decidedly inferior player, one with whom you would not be caught dead playing either now or in the foreseeable future, you can afford to be—nay, you must be—brutally dishonest. 'Thank you,' you should say coldly, as you sit there in your tennis whites twirling your racquet, 'but I'm not playing today.' You should then arrange any game you are able to arrange so that the decidedly inferior player will see that you are too playing today. He will never have the temerity to approach you again. Should you be tempted to be softhearted, remember that you are sternly disciplining him for his own good." Here again, the Professor peels off a card from his seemingly inexhaustible supply: *"No tennis player can enjoy the happy camaraderie that tennis offers until he has learned his proper place."*

"You have now mastered the two basic principles upon which all tennis matches depend," concludes the Professor, "how to arrange a game and how to avoid a game. All that remains is to learn how best to hit the ball over the net between the white lines. You will find this relatively simple."

The Professor invariably insists that a beginning pupil, after learning—*dadada-rup!*—to pick up the ball, wait a minimum of sixty days before returning for the second lesson.

"One hopes," the Professor commences, after removing the cigar from his mouth, "that you have now learned the rudiments of how to arrange a game. If you have applied yourself you should be able to hit the ball not only forth, but, on many occasions, back. You are already superior, then, to many other players. Thus, you must now master the second fundamental of tennis, a fundamental that will stand you in good stead all of your tennis-playing life, to wit: how to avoid a game."

Here, the Professor replaces his cigar and peels off another yellow card. It reads: *"All tennis players are invariably off their game."*

"Kindly commit this to memory." he says, pausing

to wait for the pupil's nodded signal of compliance. "There is one member of the club, who shall remain nameless (Doc Pritchgart), who is eighty-three years old and who has been off his game for three quarters of a century. Please note that whenever a tennis player misses a shot, he will respond in one or more of the following seven manners: one, he will frown, indicating surprise that a player of his caliber could have failed to convert such an easy opportunity into a blistering winner; two, he will curse, indicating his conviction that the gods are arrayed against him for mysterious reasons of their own; three, he will hold the racquet up in front of his face in order to examine it, presumably to make sure he remembered to have it strung before carrying it onto the court; four, after hitting a ground stroke into the net or fence, he will freeze into immobility at the end of his follow-through in order to demonstrate his classic form and obvious fact that the blame, therefore, lies with the elements, fate, or anyone in the vicinity but himself; five, he will clutch his elbow, shoulder, wrist, knee or whatever part of his anatomy is currently causing him suffering to show that if he had not been in agonizing pain, he would have executed a perfect shot; six, he will drop his racquet with a clatter to show his disgust with the way he is playing, his partner, his opponents, the game of tennis in general, or life itself; or, seven, he will simply hurl his racquet at the net, fence, or sky. This suggests he is angry.

"In any one of these cases, it matters not a whit that the player has missed precisely the same shot on several thousand previous occasions. If he were on his game, he would have made it. As every player invariably misses dozens of shots in every match, every player is, *ipso facto*, invariably off his game. The underlying cause for this phenomenon is not difficult to unearth."

Now the Professor peels off still another card: *"Every tennis player honestly and sincerely believes that he is a far better tennis player than he actually is."*

"I assume," continues the Professor when the pupil has memorized this maxim, "that you have observed the framed admonishment over the bar which states, 'Members will please refrain from challenging superior players'? I will concede that no member would dare commit such a breach of etiquette. The problem arises with the lesser player who believes he is better than he is and thus also believes he is as good as you—you who naturally believe you are better than you are. The danger of accepting the challenge of this lesser player lies not only in the damage it will do to your social standing to be seen playing with him, but in the threat that he may defeat you if you are off your game. And, as you are always off your game, this is a distinct possibility.

"On the surface, the solution to avoiding a game would appear simple. You merely offer some polite excuse such as, 'Thank you, I'd love to play if I hadn't just broken my left leg in three places above the knee.' This would indicate you didn't wish to play. But you do wish to play. You wish to play with someone else. And should you subsequently inveigle a superior player into a match, the inferior player you avoided would be fully justified in shouting from the sidelines as you reach up to smash away an easy lob, 'Leg feeling better?' This may cause you to miss the shot and put you further off your game, which you are already off."

At this point, the Professor places his cigar in his mouth and peels off one of his little yellow cards. It reads: *"No tennis player, no matter what his caliber, wants to play tennis with any other tennis player who is not better than he."*

"Kindly commit this to memory," says the Professor, pausing to allow the pupil to do so. "Excellent. Now you see that the primary art of tennis is not in playing the game, but in arranging a game. At this very moment, millions of tennis players are hitting the ball back and forth over nets between white lines. And precisely half of them wish they were playing with someone else.

"First of all, they are not improving their games. More important, they are handicapping themselves in the critical art of arranging future games. For if they are seen playing with inferior players, superior players with whom they wish to play will identify them with the inferior players with whom they are playing and will never invite them to play. Worse yet, players slightly inferior to the inferior players with whom they are playing will make the same identification and will besiege them with invitations to play. Such a path can only lead inexorably downward to the depths of degradation.

"How, then, do you, a rank beginner, surmount this initial challenge of finding someone with whom to play? Your first step, obviously, is to disguise the fact that you are a rank beginner. This requires the proper equipment, with which Miss Agnes will supply you following our lesson today.

"Meanwhile, we will turn to mastering the essential skills of tennis.

"As you may have noticed at social occasions such as cocktail parties and the like, tennis players mysteriously gravitate to each other. Once the conversation turns to tennis, as it inevitably does, they begin sniffing and circling, each trying to determine whether the other is superior or inferior and should therefore be challenged or avoided. The handicaps of tennis players, unlike those of golfers, are known only to God and those with whom they have played. Thus the opening gambit is invariably, 'Where do you play?' You should reply, 'Oh, here and there.' You will be asked if you have ever played with so-and-so or so-and-so, in an attempt to find a mutual opponent to serve as a standard. As you have never played with anyone, this will fail. The only possible ploy remaining is the question, 'How do you pick up the ball?' If you say you bend over and pick it up with your hand, the average player will switch the conversation to the stock market and go look for an ashtray. If you say you lift it up between your racquet and the side of your foot, he might conceivably invite you to play mixed doubles. But — ah! — if you coolly announce that you merely tap the ball rapidly with the strings of your racquet—*dadada-rup!*—causing it to leap up into your waiting hand, he will immediately put you down as a top-flight player and cleverly inveigle you into a match he will loathe. By attending enough cocktail parties, you will rapidly improve your game.

"That concludes our first lesson."

Should the pupil be so bold as to ask for a demonstration on the proper method of picking up a ball, the Professor will light his cigar, stare off into space, and say, as always, "One learns by doing, not watching. Go practice, practice, practice."

An initial insight into the Tiddling Tennis Theorem can be gained through the first lesson the Professor gives to rank beginners. It hasn't varied by a comma in the past ten years, nor has his delivery, which approaches a disinterested monotone:

"So you have decided to take up tennis. A marvelous decision. You couldn't have chosen a sport with more to offer: concentrated exercise, intellectual challenge, inexpensive equipment, and a new circle of friends who will provide lifelong companionship. Of course, as in all sports, there are difficulties to surmount. The first difficulty you will encounter is that no one wants to play with you."

Two factors distinguished the Professor from every other tennis instructor in the country. One was his unorthodox teaching methods, which he claimed were based on the Tiddling Tennis Theorem. He would begin each half-hour lesson, for which he now charged $10, by removing from his pocket a stack of yellow cards. On each was printed a different maxim. These were known collectively as "Roberts' Rules of Order." With great care, he would unwind the rubber band that embraced them and hand the top card to his student. "Kindly commit this to memory," he would say. When the student nodded to signify this task had been accomplished, the Professor would then deliver a fifteen-minute lecture on the meaning and ramifications of that day's maxim. For the remainder of the half hour, the Professor would stand at the net tossing balls from a shopping cart at his side to his eagerly swinging pupil.

But what established the Professor's uniqueness as a tennis instructor beyond doubt was the fact that he had never been seen to hit a tennis ball nor, for that matter, to hold a tennis racquet in his hand. A few disgruntled members, led by Doc Pritchgart, argued that the Professor didn't know *how* to hit a tennis ball and should be fired, therefore, as a disgrace to his profession. The other disgruntled members (all members of the Tiddling Tennis Club were disgruntled) felt, however, that the proof was in the pudding and the success of the Professor's brainchild—the Tiddling Tennis Theorem—could not be gainsaid.

What was odd about the Tiddling Tennis Theorem was that the Professor steadfastly refused to divulge its nature. When pressed to the extreme, he would respond gruffly, "No researcher of repute publishes his findings until they have been proven experimentally. I have not yet had the opportunity to conduct my final experiment." Most of his students merely accepted the existence and workings of the Tiddling Tennis Theorem on faith, taking comfort, as do we all, from the belief they were being guided by a higher law.

A Word from Our Commentator

**TOM
CARTER**

(The number of tennis tournaments carried on television has increased steadily. A large share of the telecasting has fallen to Flip Jones, an alumnus of the Ted Baxter School of Broadcasting. And now, down to courtside . . .)

The World Championship of Tennis finals have just concluded and Hunt Stadium is still buzzing. The TV camera pans the crowd and swings down to courtside where we are told that our colorful commentator has cornered the winner. The reflections from the camera lights gleam on Flip's pate above his fashionable shoulder-length hair. He wears a modern beige and gray, Rorschach-design, fiberglass astronaut jump suit that's so popular in tennis circles these days.

Flip is on camera now. Presumably, Ken is at his side.

Flip: Yes, folks, this has been the greatest moment in tennis. Little Kenny Rosewall, the crafty little master from Down Under who used to carry acorns to class with him as a kid because his pockets were too small for tennis balls: the ingenious David who has been slaying brutal Goliaths for three incredible decades; the quiet Dorian Gray and son of a hamster-shop owner from Sydney has once again won the richest prize in tennis—one million dollars here in Dallas' mammoth Hunt Stadium where the scorching sun can fry eggs to order in the doubles alleys.

Kenny was down 31 match points—count them—20 in the fifth set alone—and miraculously imposed his iron will on Rodney Rocket, the bandy-legged, red-haired Rocket who has been his pesky arch-rival for longer than most tennis fans can remember.

Yes, Muscles, as Hop used to call him because the undernourished 140-pounder was a fugitive from Charles Atlas ads, raced through the draw and creamed the rising young milk-fed talent, smashed the great Emmo, dazzled the Flying Dutchman, defanged Dracula and clipped Godzilla's wings and finally— finally in that final to end all finals—he defused the Rocket.

Now, Kenny...

(Jones turns quickly to Rosewall but can't find him. That's because Rosewall has decided to sit down on the court. He gets up wearily.)

Flip: Kenny, now tell us just how you feel after this stirring climax to your career that started so long ago on a rutted, dirt court in a middle-class Sydney neighborhood. You must feel great! Did you call Wilma and the kids?

Ken: Well, Flip, it's always a privilege to be able to play in a fine tournament such as this event...

Flip: Yes, yes, Kenny, you've made 11 appearances here and defied and humiliated the world's brainiest computers by winning every single one, but none as breathtaking as this one... I saw a stockbroker on the first row swallow a beer bottle... And incidentally, your bank roll has come to make Lamar's look like the federal minimum wage. What are you going to do with all the money, bury it in your yard in a rusty oil drum?

Ken: Pardon?

Flip: The money, Kenny, what are you going to do with it? And that Gibraltar-sized diamond ring Lamar gave you—I saw them bring it in and it's the first time I've seen a steam shovel get a hernia. Fred and Sedg and Emmo and Newk say you might buy another hotel chain—or a round of beer. Have you decided which?

Ken: Well, Flip, you know traveling takes a lot of expenses. But I don't have any plans outside of school clothes for the boys.

Flip: I'm sure a lot of viewers would like to know how a 48-year-old man who has immortalized himself on the tennis courts since those great Davis Cup days 30 years ago can keep winning all the big ones and play only once a week. What's your secret? Vitamins? Yoga? Prayer? That breakfast cereal you eat?

Ken: Well, Flip, I think it's important to watch the

ball well, and there's a little exercise...

Flip: Indeed, and that's exactly what you did today when you finally reached your first and only match point against the fiery Rocket. And you passed him with the classic backhand, cleanly threading the tiniest, most microscopic needle. It's got to be the most fabulous shot in tennis. Tell me, what were you thinking when you hit it?

Ken: As you say, it was my first time at match point in my favor so I tried to concentrate, Flip. But actually, the backhand wasn't necessarily my best shot today.

Flip: Well, I know it wasn't bourbon or Scotch! You keep in top condition even though you're merely a weekend player now, and you seldom quaff anything but beer, and then two's your limit—and it has always been that way even when pro tennis struggled along: a tiny, heroic band of renegade pros puttering across the countryside in a battered cream and green '49 Ford station wagon whose windows wouldn't even work, to say nothing of the glove compartment, and playing in stinking, drafty barns with floors warped so badly you thought you were on a roller coaster—and you were there. Kenny Rosewall, believing in a pro game amidst a universe of doubters, putting your reputation on the line every night for peanuts because you loved the game, working your Trojan heart out when there seemed no light at the end of the bleak tunnel...

(Jones pauses to catch his breath.)

Ken: Yes, Flip, I guess there aren't many of the oldtimers left anymore. But I've found a curious thing about the aging process...

Flip: And I know that whatever your secret is, Kenny, it will take you ever higher in tennis—gosh, if that's possible—and you'll be right back here next year defending the title against all the starry-eyed young talent and the grim, seasoned pros. Right now—tell us—what are your immediate plans?

Ken: Well, Flip, I thought I'd take a shower...

(With that, Jones steps in front of him to face the camera.)

Flip: And all tennisdom knows, it's a well-deserved

one for little Kenny, the fantastic former choir boy who marched through this super bowl like Sherman took Georgia. It may have taken Handel 14 days to write "The Messiah," but it took the gutsy little master just six to pull down the richest prize in tennis. Limping slightly from a difficult knee operation and coming from behind in virtually all other matches, he emerged smelling like a rose.

Now, this is Flip Jones reminding you to join us here next week at the same time for a special interview with Harry Hopman, the craggy-faced but brilliant former Australian Davis Cup coach who used to make the champion practice speaking with marbles in his mouth to rid him of a stuttering habit that often confused his practice opponents . . .

(At this point an ill-timed aspirin ad cuts in.)

Swinging with the Stars

DAVID WILTSE

It all started one November when TENNIS magazine ran an article of mine in which I made fun of myself and a low-level celebrity tennis tournament I had somehow been invited to enter. A few weeks later, to my astonishment, I received a Mailgram from Bill Cosby—one of the most prominent of the celebrity tennis players—challenging me to a singles match in Las Vegas. I had never met Cosby, and all I knew about him as a tennis player was that he was supposed to be very good. His motive, I assumed, was to give me a good-natured thrashing for having suggested that celebrity tennis isn't a gripping spectator sport.

My first response, as always in times of tension, was to dash out and eat lots of refined sugar. My second response was to tell my wife, Nancy. "Bill Cosby!" she said. "He's supposed to be very good, isn't he? I hear he's a great athlete." That was the first note of what became a leitmotif for the next several months. I heard "he's very good, he's a great athlete" so often that I began to believe he'd won the decathlon at the Olympics just before Bruce Jenner. It did not escape my notice that no one said: "Cosby? He's very good, *but* so are you. You can take him."

The more I heard of Cosby's prowess, the more unhinged I became. It was whispered that the man held a racquet in each hand, that Howard Cosell had dubbed him as good as any pro, that he told jokes while waiting for lobs to descend. After a few weeks of that, my tension level was so high my wife suggested I take a stress test to see if I could survive the match.

Then, I did something sensible—I screamed for help. My two excellent local Connecticut pros, Steve Campbell of the Weston Racquet Club, and Gene Chappell of Norwalk Indoor Tennis, gave generously of their time and expertise. Campbell worked with me on my favorite Har-Tru surface, trying to develop some consistency and depth to my strokes. Chappell drilled me in serve and volley to get me ready for the fast Las Vegas court where I'd meet Cosby.

Despite their best efforts, I felt we were applying a Band-aid to an internal hemorrhage. The opponent I feared most was not Cosby but that wide-eyed, terrified little boy in training pants who lurks inside me and grabs the controls at the first sign of trouble.

With that little boy protesting every step of the way, my wife and I headed for Las Vegas in early March. Just to make sure I wouldn't get any sleep while I was preparing for the match, we took our two preschool daughters along.

Las Vegas was like a cinder in the eye. Blink as I might, it wouldn't go away. Was I really in the capital of decadence to play *tennis?* I had organized my training to peak at just the right moment, like a vintage wine grape, and now I was surrounded by people who gambled, stayed up late, drank and wore little silver spoons around their necks.

My notion of Spartan conditioning was offended. After all, I'd been dieting for three months and dropped at least a pound. Remembering how John Newcombe had prepared for a Wimbledon bid by running up a hill again and again and again, I had begun to take the garbage out instead of stalling until my wife did it. I recalled how Bobby Riggs had dosed himself with megavitamins for his match with Billie Jean King. Not knowing what else to take, I consumed large quantities of Vitamin C. At the worst, I figured I wouldn't have scurvy for the big match.

On our arrival, Cosby was most gracious. He saw to it that I had everything I wanted. What I really wanted, but didn't mention, was a security blanket. He gave me the next best thing, a coach. My mentor for the big match was George McCall, the tennis director at the Sands Hotel and a former U.S. Davis Cup captain.

Let me get right to the heart of the matter: George McCall was a prince to me. He saw immediately that he had charge of a scared chick and he took me under his wing in the warmest, gentlest, most comforting way possible. He gave me instruction, he gave me advice, he gave me the feeling I was in good hands. Best of all, he gave me the feeling that I was no longer solely responsible for myself; and a good thing, too, because I'd had me for years and look at the mess I'd made.

I secluded myself in my garishly tasteful hotel room, avoiding the gambling, but Vegas has other ways to get to your mind. The day before the match, I was practicing my strokes in front of the mirror with the baby sitting on my foot, when suddenly came the Great Revelation! I'd been swinging the racquet all wrong! Just two weeks earlier, I'd been at the Colony Beach & Tennis Resort in Sarasota where Nick Bollettieri (Brian Gottfried's coach) had worked with me for a few days. The gist of Bollettieri's comments was that I was too stiff and tight, and didn't move well.

Now, looking in the mirror, I realized that I was too stiff and tight, and didn't move well! I had believed, but I hadn't understood. Now, I knew! And even better, I knew how to fix it. All that was required was a complete overhaul of my swing, beginning with the ready position. Could I do it all in 12 hours? If I skipped breakfast, why not?

Oh, Las Vegas. Even the mirrors are seductive.

As I walked to the indoor courts of the Tropicana Hotel on the day of the match, the little boy within was working himself into a frenzy. A man stopped me and said he had agreed with my article. He, too, was sick of all this celebrity stuff (by which I knew he hadn't read the article).

"As far as I'm concerned," he said, "you've got nothing to lose. You're playing him on his home court, he's got the best coaches in the country, he's been playing for years, he can afford to play all the time and with the best available partners, he's used to being in front of crowds and cameras . . . ."

"Cameras?" I croaked. My intestines shriveled within me.

"If you lose 6-4, 6-4," he went on, "it's a moral

victory for you."

The little boy within me asked: "But what if I lose 6-0, 6-0?"

"Well, that's possible," he said. "I hear he's very good."

With this reminder of Cosby's excellence, I walked onto the court to warm up with McCall. There was an audience of about 100 people and, sure enough, cameras. Stay loose, I told myself. Move your feet, swing easy, keep the ball in play.

"Run while you have the chance!" said the little boy. "Sprain your ankle! Fall and foam at the mouth! But do it quickly before you start to weep with hysteria." With this little dialogue going on in my head, we warmed up for half an hour. In that time, I hit three balls into the court. I swear to you, *three* balls.

"You're looking good, you're swinging well," said McCall.

"But none of the balls went in!" I piped.

"Now just relax," my wife kept telling me, her voice cracking. "I'll still love you, no matter what." (That was the first time I realized my marriage was on the line.) "The worst thing that can happen is you'll lose a tennis match."

"Use your imagination!" the little boy shrieked. "I could get killed! I could lose every single point! I could double fault 24 straight times!"

Suddenly a crowd of people sauntered onto the court, chatting amiably. They dispersed into the linesmen's chairs. Then, children in short pants came out and gamboled, tossing balls back and forth. What was this, a picnic? Why were all these people here? An umpire climbed into the elevated chair, putting the final seal of legitimacy on the event—or hammering the last nail into my coffin, if you prefer.

Playing tennis with the full complement of officials and ball boys is at least three times as difficult as playing without them. Counting linesmen, ball boys, coaches, wives and hangers-on, there were 20 people on the court, listening to me mutter: "Jerk, get the ball over the net." With everyone sitting or standing around, it was like having a match in the parlor with all the family gathered. It was hard to think. Easy to panic, natural to blubber—but hard to think.

How did Cosby react to it? Cosby is a very experienced player. He has been entering junior veteran tournaments for three years. He has played in many pro-celebrity tournaments, some of them on television. I'm unable to say for sure that he wasn't nervous, but I did notice his shirt never came untucked. Either he had it taped to his thighs, or I never made him stretch. I looked like I'd just lost a wrestling match after our warmup, and he never perspired.

The match finally began. Cosby threw in a big serve and came to the net. My mind yelled: flee! My body, however, had turned to stone. While my brain ran off and hid behind the net post, my body clanked around like an empty suit of armor. I was not a nervous wreck, for wreck implies something is salvageable. I was a nervous ruin.

After the first game, I came to the bench, panting with tension. "You returned well, under the circumstances," said McCall. The circumstances were that I didn't get a return over the net. He wiped off my racquet handle and sent me back out, telling me: "Don't let him rest. Press him." That was to be the pattern of the match. While I was doing my best just to breathe, Cosby was having a jolly conversation on his bench. But I kept pressing him.

Later, I learned that McCall didn't want me to have time to think about things. A good tactic, but three months too late.

In the second game, when I served and finally won a point, I learned another aspect of playing before a crowd: they take sides. When Cosby hit a winner or I made an error, there was a loud chorus of cheering for him. When I won a point, there was a deathly silence, as if I'd done something in rather bad taste and everyone was overlooking it.

Now, being cheered against is something you don't normally encounter in daily life. People don't yell: "Yeah, Fred, you loused up the books!" It hurts your feelings and confirms a secret suspicion that the whole world's against you.

The score reached 5-4 in the first set, my serve, and an awful thought occurred to me. I could win! McCall was right about not letting me think, but he should have muzzled the umpire as well. There the man sat, reminding me in funereal tones that, in effect, "You are ahead, you have the serve, it is up to you to win it or lose it." There has never been a more damaging message. I did what I'd been rehearsing for weeks, what anyone with a lead casing on his serving arm would do. I lost the game at love, then proceeded to lose the set in a tiebreaker.

The second set was a repeat of the first. Cosby won the second tiebreaker and the match 7-6, (7-2), 7-6, (10-8).

Afterward, during a talk with Cosby, I got the big surprise. Cosby had not been joking. The challenge had been issued in some pique following a series of articles knocking celebrity tennis, of which mine was just the last straw. Which is not to say he took me seriously. The match no longer mattered, he said, "once I saw your strokes." I felt that statement was best left unexamined.

So how good a tennis player is Bill Cosby? By whose standards? The comic doesn't consider himself "a real tennis player." He is constantly working on his game and is determined to improve, but right now, by his own admission, he's a good club player, nothing more.

As for me, to compound my perversities, I found that all the tension was stimulating—like walking into an electric fence. It's habit-forming and I'm ready for more. Bring on Bruce Jenner!

"What'ya mean, 'We can't win every set,'... we haven't won any!"

"When it isn't reviving tennis balls, I use it to keep my beer from
going flat between games."

"We lost, Charlie, because you weren't concentrating!"

"Let's work on your quickness at net."

In One Leap, He Joined the Immortals

STAN ISAACS

In 1962, the year-end reviews record Sonny Liston beat Floyd Patterson; *Weatherly* won a boat race; Rod Laver picked up all the tennis balls; the Yankees won big and the Mets lost even bigger. But what did the year-end reviews tell us about Anthony Lieberman?

Nothing. In all the fustian and whim wham about the world of fun and games, nobody recalled the short moment of glory of Anthony Lieberman.

You ask, "Who is Anthony Lieberman?" Ah, let a kindergarten scholar of footnotes to history tell about him. In the ranks of men who had greatness thrust upon them, there always should be a place for Anthony Lieberman.

Let us wake up the echoes. The place is the Oritani Field Club in Hackensack, New Jersey. It is a balmy day in June and Anthony Lieberman of Philadelphia is playing Sidney Schwartz of Queens in the second round of the Eastern clay courts tennis championships.

Schwartz—you might call him the "Fast Sidney" of the New York tennis circuit—is ranked No. 1 in this tournament, but he is on the verge of defeat against the sturdy unknown Philadelphian.

Schwartz won the first set, 6-1, then lost the second, 6-0. He is behind, 5-3, in the final set. Lieberman is serving at 40-30, match point.

In Lieberman's words, "It was my serve. I gave him a twist serve that took him off the court at his backhand. His return was a soft, high bounce left of center. I was coming in toward the net. I jumped and hit a high backhand shot that took him off the court at his forehand. I didn't figure he'd be able to go for it, let alone get it."

So Lieberman, with the momentum of his rush to the net, continued running and leaped over the net in that inimitable tennis gesture, ready to shake hands and accept congratulations from the loser. As long as that gesture is in tennis, it will be a gentleman's game.

But Fast Sidney Schwartz forgot to offer congratulations. Instead, he was running furiously to the side of the court to return the shot. Miraculously, maybe, Schwartz got his racquet on the ball. "He's a pretty agile fellow; he runs fast," Lieberman said. Schwartz's ball lofted high in the air, went over the net, and plopped to earth Lieberman never dreamed where—on his side of the court.

Lieberman, a victory-less conqueror, gulped. Here, the two combatants' memory of the event conflicts. "He was breathless," Schwartz said. "He sat there with a despondent grin. He didn't want to talk. He said he was overanxious."

"I knew exactly what had happened," Lieberman said. "I told him, 'Nice shot.' I was being carried by my momentum toward the net and kept going because I didn't think he would get the ball. Even if I had not jumped over, I wouldn't have been able to get his return shot."

Under the rules, it didn't matter whether Schwartz's return shot was in or not. A player is not allowed to leave his side of the net until his shot has taken a second bounce. Lieberman disqualified himself by jumping before Schwartz's ball bounced. He was a dead clay-court pigeon.

"There were about 200 people in the stands," Schwartz said, "and I thought they would all fall out of the stands. They were doubled up howling."

To complete the story, Schwartz came back to tie the score and win the set and the match. He also went on to win the tournament. The next day, Schwartz "received telephone calls from everybody who knew me." None of them would believe it actually had happened, he said.

On the phone yesterday, Lieberman said, "The Philadelphia papers didn't make too much fuss about it," for which he seemed glad. His friends kidded him about it for a few weeks, he admitted. Though it is more than six months later, the young man still seemed embarrassed about it.

He shouldn't be. He should learn to bask in the greatness that has been thrust upon him. Had Lieberman not been moved by that certain something which lifts a man out of the ranks of the multitude to a place with the titans, he might merely have won the point,

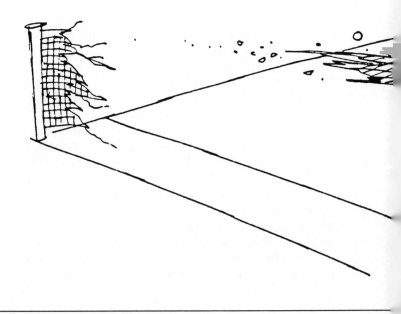

the match—and maybe even gone on to win the tournament.

But what is a tournament to the higher glory resulting from Lieberman's Leap? Leaping across the net into the hearts of sportsmen everywhere, Anthony Lieberman enriched the sports year of 1962. Not Liston nor Laver, nor even Marv Throneberry did more.

"What's the word, dear, for when my shot just skims the net and dies suddenly in your court?"

Strange How Tennis Has Changed

ELLIOT CHAZE

Recently, and temporarily, I despaired of golf and on a glistening hot afternoon decided to resume a habit known as tennis.

In tennis the addict moves about a hard rectangle and seeks to ambush a fuzzy ball with a modified snow-shoe. There is a net in the middle of the court and often you can find the ball at the base of this net—a convenience denied golfers.

The primary conception of tennis is to get the ball over the net and at the same time to keep it within bounds of the court; failing this, within the borders of the neighborhood.

For the man of years there are three main strokes: forehand, backhand and sun.

Before this account attains full focus I wish to call attention to the fact I had not played the game for six years. I had not played it well in twenty and maybe I never did. Like the man said, I'm not the man I used to be and never *was*. I have been smoking two packages of cigarettes daily and trying to break in a rack of pipes which my wife believes are becoming to, if not manda-tory for, a writer.

Also, I am so extravagantly built, despite sporadic dieting, that when I brake to a dead halt in rubber-soled shoes my middle slings forward long after the feet are stilled. During ensuing moments, centrifugal force and retraction tear at the flesh beneath my T-shirt and I may be said to shimmy.

With what amounted to less than cunning I chose as my opponent for this afternoon a man who neither smokes, drinks nor shimmies.

He too is plump, but his burden is more wholesome and disciplined. It moves with him in whatever direction he desires and does not seem in any way to conflict with his footwork or breathing.

During the preliminary warm-up I discovered that to indulge in the habit of tennis one must run many times, never very far in any single direction, but continuously in countless directions. This had slipped my mind. I'd recalled simply the striking of the ball from various, rather photogenic, angles; transportation didn't enter into it at all. You were here. You were there. You hit the ball. Now and then you called out, "Fine shot, beautiful, really!"

The truth is (and heed this if you plan renewal of the game you enjoyed as a colt), you must strain every valve and vessel to the limit of its guaranty to earn the privilege of hacking at the ball. Indeed, you must swim rivers of sweat, burn scarlet scabs on your nose in the sun and run, run, run. And I don't mean the whimsical or gracious kind of running one does from patio to telephone.

Gone is the insolent floating grace of yesteryear, the light clean loping and hard-curving stroke. After slogging eight desperate paces to meet the ball you're too whacked to care if the shot is crisp and well placed.

And the serve.

Remember the glow you used to get when your service came around, the fresh steel of forearm, shoulder and calf? You didn't even have to think about it. You pondered your suntan, your date for the evening and the achingly beautiful prospect of Swiss steak and butter beans for supper.

Sometimes you barely realized you'd served until the ball hissed over the taped rim of the net.

That's all different now, I find.

When I cranked up, there was a bleak crunch in the working shoulder, the sort of thing one hears when cutting a deck of lettuce with the edge of a fork.

Simply getting up high on the ball of the left foot proved a test of balance and calf sinew, the racquet handle slick in my fist, eyes stinging with the fluids of exhaustion.

Twice I threw the ball too high and lost it in the sun

on my service. Someone snickered on the next court. I believe it was a teen-age girl for whom I'd been trying to hold in my stomach. There is no question she had a right to laugh. On another occasion I tossed up two balls at once and stepped on the third and did a quarter-split.

At game's end my companion leaped the net the way they do in the newsreels and without looking me in the eye said he was tired. "Let's take a break," he said. "It's hot out here." He breathed evenly and moved all of a piece and there was barely a button of sweat on him.

I tried to smile. "All right."

We walked to a wooden practice wall at the end of the line of courts and sat down, leaning against the wood, he still trying manfully to look exhausted, neither of us saying much; and it hit me then with a sorrowful slap what time had done to a machine which only a handful of years ago had brimmed with energy and careless strength. Suddenly one day you leaned against a wooden wall and knew you were a slob.

Nevertheless, I may—I'm not pledging myself, but I just may—try it again. I have thought it out at length and believe that if comfort and self-satisfaction are the things that destroy a man, tennis might well be the key to eternal health.

"He's doing much better since I changed targets."

"He's in training for Saturday's tennis tournament.
He's going to be a linesman."

Tales of a Wimbledon Linesman

**ALAN
KENYON**

I crouched forward in my chair, causing it to tilt forward precariously, and peered down the outside service line of court No. 5. My back hurt from this less than dignified position and, by comparison, weeding in my back garden began to take on a rosy hue. At least when I'm bending there, I don't have to suddenly lunge sideways because of momentarily blocked vision! However, this was Wimbledon, I reminded myself, and how few come even to walk on the hallowed turf let alone sit on it. Anyway, Neale Fraser was about to serve. This was no time for second thoughts.

"Whack" and simultaneously, or so it seemed, Rex Hartwig pulled his racquet away from a ball that missed the line by a hairsbreadth and crashed into the green backdrop beside me. "Fault," I screamed, reminding myself of the first commandment for linesmen: "Thou shalt not whisper." I was determined, come what may, not to reveal my newness by committing such a cardinal sin.

A hush fell over the crowd. Had I frightened them I wondered? No, Fraser had stopped in mid-serve. One serve gone, and here he was striding toward the net. Perhaps Hartwig had offended him? Made a rude sign? Said a naughty word? No. Fraser mentally brushed his opponent aside and glared at me. I immediately felt at a certain disadvantage. He was standing with both hands on the net cord and glaring. I was sitting with both hands on my knees and simply wondering. The suspense didn't last long.

"Just because he (Hartwig) lets the ball go through, doesn't mean you have to call it a fault," he snarled.

Now, I thought to myself, feeling the hairs on the back of my neck bristling, if you made a similar accusation of a lack of professionalism to a garbage collector or a bus driver, you'd have some kind of trouble on your hands. Probably a strike. But linesmen don't have unions, I reminded myself sadly. I cast my mind, with not a little tenderness, to the sage who has already expressed the view that when a player becomes aggressive, why don't all the umpires—who give up so much of their time to work for nothing, generally not even thanks—just get up and leave. Let him sort it out for himself. So I quietly remained seated and basked in this pacifying reflection.

However, it wasn't long before I was snapped out of my reverie. At the change of ends, Fraser came up to me and said loudly: "You're calling too slow!"

This time the situation was too much for me. My reaction overcame my discretion. "This is the Grand Masters," I muttered. "We're all a little slower than we used to be."

It was obvious from the look I got that Fraser didn't particularly appreciate the remark. I, for my part, said a quiet prayer for the fact that this was a quarterfinal in the Grand Masters (over 45's) event and not his Wimbledon singles final of 18 years before. After all, surely he must have mellowed a little since then!

How had I, an Australian expatriate living in Paris, come to be calling lines at Wimbledon? Well, some time before I had joined the Lawn Tennis Umpires Association of Great Britain. My credentials for entry had been a letter of recommendation from the president of my tennis club, a background of tennis playing and umpiring stretching to the sunny days of Australian tennis in the 1950's, and youth! Age 40 in this field is a fledgling.

Then, when rain washed out a good portion of the first week's play last year, there was such a hefty backlog of matches that more officials were needed. I presented myself at the association, was eagerly accepted by the supervisor of Wimbledon umpires and proudly walked away with a circular blue Wimbledon official's lapel badge. I was told to be at the All England Club an hour before play was to start on Monday of the tournament's second week.

Duly presenting myself, I was given a card with the

"daily order of play" on the Centre Court and the other 14 courts, and a slip of paper asking Kenyon (me!) to "please take a line on the 1st, 3rd and 5th matches on Court No. 9." Oh well, I hadn't really expected to draw the Centre or No. 1 Court right away and, anyway, there was a footnote saying that "linesmen on Centre and No. 1 Courts must take their places immediately on going into Court and remain seated during warm-up." It did sound a little formal and I thought I'd probably be more at home on No. 9.

I put my head down and with a resolute air set about fighting my way past, so it seemed, every one of the 300,000 people who come to Wimbledon in any one year, to get to Court 9!

My list informed me that the first match would be between Tom Okker and Tom Leonard. A fourth round of the men's singles. A nice match to begin with. Okker is such a little fellow that, I thought, even if I am a little nervous there won't be anything to worry about in that direction. (I remembered the anecdote reputedly attributed to Okker that on being asked how he changed his game in windy conditions, he said he tried hard to remain upright on the court.) The other Tom was less familiar; in fact, I didn't know him at all. I waited impatiently—naively as it turned out—to make his acquaintance.

As midday approached, the players appeared and started their warm-up but I was still alone. That did give me a moment's apprehension. It was obvious I was new, because I needn't have worried. A few minutes later five uniformed gentlemen pushed their way through the gathering crowd and I went up to them. "Are you Kenyon?" I was asked. "We've been wondering where you were." I learned that I should have assembled at the central umpires' office. My newness was showing again.

We milled around the umpire with the score sheet and I listened to a code that, on the spur of the moment, sounded like something the Kremlin would have been proud of. "Mr. Brown, NT; Mr. Smith, FT; Mr. Jones, MS; Mr. Kenyon, LB," etc. I was perplexed and, sensing that, a kindly-faced old gentleman sidled up to me and whispered, "LB means left baseline, next to me." I felt and looked very grateful and took my seat. Now the code was broken, the others fell into place; NT, Near Tram (near sideline); FT, Far Tram (far sideline); MS, Moving Service (the service line both ends). It could only get easier from now on.

I had reckoned without the players. In addition to their Christian names, they shared one other thing in common: disdain for all officials. For example, shortly after the match began, Okker from the far end told me and a few hundred others, that my call of "out" on his drive was the worst call he had ever witnessed in his life.

I felt that was a little unkind on two counts, even though it was my first match. One, he was at the *other* end and I was calling the baseline in front of me. And two, even with my lack of experience at Wimbledon, I couldn't believe, with all the matches played here and elsewhere every year, that I could have established a record of ineptitude so quickly and so emphatically. But he was in no doubt and reiterated the charge when he changed ends.

Oh dear, I thought, If this is umpiring at Wimbledon, I'll probably set another record—that one for brevity of service!

Later, when Okker doubted a service call and asked Leonard to refer to the service linesman, Leonard snapped: "Don't disturb him, he's sleeping."

Finally, to my relief, the match ended with Okker winning in three sets and it was apparently time for lunch. MS told me I should eat now since it might be my only opportunity! But I had other plans: to return to the idyllic world of spectator, for a moment. Raul Ramirez and John Newcombe were playing on Centre Court and I was going to realize the dream of a lifetime by sitting in the umpires' section and watching a match there. I intended to take full advantage of the armchair I knew must be waiting for me.

"There's no time to watch matches here," came the rude awakening to my dream. "Remember you're an umpire now." The connection was too subtle for me and, seeing my perplexity, my friend went on:

"We've got matches 3 and 5 to do on this court. If the second match is over quickly, we're on again before you can say Fred Hoyles (the tournament referee). . . . And don't forget that umpires are expected to report to the referee's office at the end of the first set preceding their next match (or second set if it's a five-set match). We've just got time to bolt down some strawberries and cream!"

"Whew!" was my profound reply. "You mean we can never watch a match on Centre Court?"

"It has been done but it's difficult. You see, there's no way of knowing the score of the match in progress out on your court."

"There's no warning system or a courier to keep you posted?"

"Oh, no, no, nothing like that."

I cheered myself with the thought that I'd only been asked to work until Thursday. I could sit back then, on Friday and Saturday, and enjoy what would be the fruits of my labors. A tennis famine for four days but a hearty surfeit—a sort of recompense—at the weekend. I said as much.

Another balloon was quickly burst. "You can't sit in the umpires' section if you're not umpiring," my friend said.

"But you just told me it's not possible to sit when I am!" I said a little exasperated.

"That's right."

And so the day passed and, in due course, the week. Within a day or two, I was really becoming a hardened campaigner. So much so that when I finally came face to face with a tournament terror named Billie Jean King and she began to tell the crowd and umpires more or less what she thought of us all, I didn't even blink, let alone blush.

Oh yes, I did try to watch the final by sneaking into the umpires' section. But I was soon spotted by zealous fellow umpires and was asked to leave. It seemed a strange way to encourge the new blood the profession so dearly needs.

"That wasn't match point."

"The boss saw your last six matches . . . he'd like you to
quit using our racquets."

"You wouldn't believe the traction on these shoes."

"George folds under pressure."

"Your strings are too tight."

"What are some other ways you believe tennis is taking over your life?"

Teamster Tennis

**RICHARD R.
SZATHMARY**

"You lousy little creep, try one more lob like that to my backhand and I'll have your hand under a punch press."

"Keep coming up to the net like that, you worm, and you're gonna find my racquet separating your molars for you."

"Goddamn it, if you can't keep your second serve in either, then we're screwed for sure against these clowns."

No, these aren't the usual run of remarks you'll hear at public or private tennis courts around the country. But the tennis boom has recently brought some—well—strange people into the embrace of the sport. And what we have here is a rather special kind of tennis played by the knights of the road who drive the big diesel rigs, the crowd that hangs out at Tommy's Diner in Wallington, N.J., lunchtime every day. And for this hard-drinking Qeager-eating, highly-paid gang of guys who do their utmost to studiously abstain from the increased productivity the front office is perpetually demanding, "lunch hour" runs from about 11 till 2.

That's more than enough time for two cheeseburgers, a side of fries and apple pie a la, plus two or three hotly contested sets of "truckers' tennis," the ultimate modification of the game to date.

It started in the working class burg of Wallington, previously known mostly for a bakery reputed to make the best black bread in the New York metropolitan area, when the local county parks commission built tennis courts on some undeveloped parkland behind Tommy's Diner, which is on a main trucking route to New York City. Tommy's is the kind of spot that serves three eggs, home fries, toast, a little plastic container of Kraft's grape jelly and coffee for under a dollar, and where what passes elsewhere for highly priced "boeuf bourgignon" is honestly labeled "pot roast."

Only two tennis courts were constructed, but they were beauties. They offered super-cushiony playing surfaces and higher than regulation fences of heavy wire mesh. But most notably, the courts were not constructed along side each other as per usual, but rather one in front of the other. They were totally separate from each other with individual gates. Thus, to play tennis at Wallington was to insure total privacy for yourself and your partners.

It's your court and yours alone. There's no chance of being asked to chase anybody else's ball because of the high fencing separating the two courts—unless the most erratic of lobbers is playing in the next court. It's dream turf.

Also, private turf. For years, the parkland in back of Tommy's has been a parking lot for truckers on their lunch hours, guys curled up in their cabs snoozing to Merle Haggard tapes on their eight-track players.

At least that's the way it was at Tommy's until someone (nobody is exactly sure who) hopped off the high running board of his rig and scrunched his ripple-soled workboots on one of the tennis courts. Pretty soon the word spread that "maybe we should start getting some exercise on our lunch break instead of bottling it up every Sunday for the pro football games on the tube." Guys began popping into local discount stores for specials on $5 Taiwanese racquets and $1-a-can "practice balls."

As every tennis player knows before he starts playing or soon learns, style is a large and essential part of the game. So once the truckers from Tommy's saw that at last here was their very own chance to play the exact same sport as those effete snobs who run around country clubs in their underwear, they went for "style" in a big way.

Cesar Tomini, who drives a big White semi from Jersey to Hartford, showed up in his old pair of Clark's desert boots (bought in London on a two-week escorted jaunt there run by his parish's Holy Name Association) and gold football pants with two purple stripes down each leg. He'd change in his truck cab and hop down to assorted cheers and boos for his grasp of the essentials of court dress.

But then his helper, Artie Melgrave, topped that with a bowling shirt from Ernie's Discount Wines & Liquors and an old pair of green-and-white hounds tooth doubleknit trousers cut off at the knees. Other truckers new to the game stuck to the "basic" court dress of green work shirt and matching pants with steel-toed, ankle-high, fawn-colored work shoes—all of which they complemented with such items as teamsters Union buttons, garrison belts with buckles commemorating old rodeos held in obscure little towns in southwest Texas and thick wool striped hunting socks.

That, then, was the sort of crowd suddenly playing tennis out behind Tommy's. What they lacked in technique, they tried to compensate for in enthusiasm—like most of us. According to Jimmy Olearcyczk, who parks his blood red and white McLean's Lines rig behind Tommy's promptly each day at noon to get in a few quick games, "This game is something on the order of giant ping-pong." And Davey Assumption, who once hauled horse trailers out to the Locust Valley polo set on Long Island, sometimes gets careless and refers to "chukkers" instead of to "sets." But that's all right.

As Tomini always says, "O.K., so this ain't the CBS Tennis Classic. So what's the beef when we screw up a couple times on the right terminology?" Anyway, it still resembles tennis.

Yet when the boys are playing, whether it's doubles (teams composed of long distance lines vs. the short-haul day hop boys) or singles (often drivers vs. their helpers), the tennis situation at the courts is strictly clubby. And be warned: don't stop there hoping to play tennis, even when only one of the courts is occupied by truckers. Tony Gator (10 years driving Newark to Tampa) may come up to you, as I once saw him do to a pair of pretty young suburban things with matching short frosted haircuts in a sky-blue Volks one day. Tony looked in the car, hefted his $5.99 "Court Rocket" racquet, adjusted his copper bracelet, and checked out the expensive steel racquets he could see on the back seat of the car.

"Nice equipment, baby," he sneered at the driver, "and maybe I don't mean the aluminum chopsticks you play with. But right now we don't need no hausfraus going slumming on *our* courts. So split."

Not to excuse his rudeness, or his chauvinism, but on his own terms Tony felt he was speaking for his "class." Many county denizens (even in the immediate area surrounding Wallington) do think of themselves as particularly "aware" suburbanites–people for whom, say, the constantly upward-mobile philosophy espoused by New York Magazine is aimed. This attitude ticks off no end guys who've finally come around, after heavy doses of the sociological musings of Jimmy Breslin and Pete Hamill, to the fact that without them delivering vital goods and services, there would be no such society in suburbia.

The guy with the good backhand, who remembers to keep his torso straight when he makes his shots, he delivers for a liquor distributor; without him there'd be no vermouth in somebody else's martinis and no V.O. at the club buffet next week. And the guy waiting his turn to play, trying hard to decide whether or not to open up a crisp new can of balls that are Macy's own brand, he makes deliveries for a dress conglomerate that services suburbia's leading department and specialty stores. Without him on the job, you might see a lot more nudity on suburban Saturday nights than even suburbia has bargained for.

And . . . well, you get it. There's been a lot of talk lately, mostly just for show, about how tennis is being rapidly democratized, how it's moving out from the WASP-only crowd.

People who talk this way point with considerably justifiable pride to the programs being set up in inner-city areas, often moderated by such well-known and well-meaning pros as Althea Gibson and Ken Rosewall. But comparable progress in white ethnic working class neighborhoods such as Wallington is either very rare or non-existent.

For the gang from Tommy's or for their children,

the thing to do if you want to play tennis is to grab yourself a cheapo racquet and a can of balls and beat it out to the nearest public tennis court, there to hack away with pleasure if not with textbook techniques. And maybe also to beat off anybody else who crabs about wanting to use your court; because in your own terms you've come a long way, baby, just when you decide to get out there in shorts and sneaks.

Maybe, too, this has something to do with the real importance of the Billie Jean King-Bobby Riggs affair for the future of tennis, at least out here in working-mans's Jersey. "If a 55-year-old guy with bad legs who talks big and a broad with thick glasses and a snappy lip can do it, then so can I," is how I've heard it put in the Raven Lounge, a bar I frequent that is sociologically , if not physically, a long way from center court at Forest Hills. If a remark like that above works, somebody who truly cares about tennis should be able to accept it.

Even I have to admit, however, that the democratization of tennis may have gone too far when guys like my friend Cosmo take to the sport. He's 6 feet 2, about 250 pounds, and wears jeans faded to an evil moldy green with engineer's boots and a purple sweat shirt cut off at the sleeves to display triceps muscles he claims are "like a pair of high quality steel springs." Wearing his "Abortion is Murder" button pinned to the bill of his cap, he cuts quite a figure as he grips his expensively gut-strung Rawlings racquet and chews out toothpicks at a rate alarming to the fragile ecology of our national forests.

Worse yet, alas, is the fact that he drives a garbage truck for a private sanitary carting firm; his truck is usually full by the time he pulls up behind Tommy's. And the combination of a strong garbage smell and scavenging birds, with an occasional field mouse or water rat waiting on the sidelines to pounce, makes for a "total tennis environment" which only the very strong-hearted can suffer. But the truckers seem to like it, and they're in charge here a major part of the afternoon. "Just Cosmo's presence toughens us up," says Davey Assumption.

So let's leave the courts in Wallington between 11

and 2 to the truckers. They're increasing their range of experiences, and in some circles that defines education. If you do attempt to play there, don't get too upset if you're asked rather forcefully to leave during their usual playing hours.

Take the way one mixed foursome in a Grand Prix was shooed away from the parking lot recently by Tony Gator and a baseball bat. The driver of the Pontiac, Rod Laver lookalike in powder blue shirt and shorts with matching crushed hat, complained while being chased away about how "the uncouth monsters could at least sometimes let somebody else, somebody else who can at least play tennis half-decently, use the courts."

Hearing that, Cosmo was not impressed as he successfully bounced a rock off the slowly departing Grand Prix's trunk area. "I don't know what gets that ace so upset," he told me. " After all is said and done, who's got the right to say we come on any bit stronger than that guy they got in professional big-time tennis with the nickname of 'Nasty?' "

That, friends, is the sort of remark you're liable to hear when you play "truckers' tennis."

Confessions of an Indoor Tennis Bum

**STAN
DRYER**

In the icy heart of winter Harvey Wellfleet left his job as research coordinator at the Megalo Corporation and became an indoor tennis bum. Harvey decided upon this drastic change in the course of a conversation with his boss, Mr. Brisbane.

"Let me get this straight, Harvey," said Mr. Brisbane. "You do not like your fine job managing an entire section of devoted scientists and you wish to go back, sulk in a corner and play with your own rack of transistors."

"I do not like supervising people," said Harvey. "I want to do research."

"Now, Harvey," said Mr. Brisbane, "you must understand that often in this world we must do things that we don't like to do. You and I, for example, have a knack with people. Therefore our smooth-running social system has placed us in positions of supervision. It is necessary for the stability of the system that we do not fight this inevitability."

"To hell with the stability of our social order," said Harvey. "I want to do what I enjoy."

"Now that isn't always possible, is it?" said Mr. Brisbane. "If you really wanted to do what you enjoy, why don't you play tennis full time at that fancy tennis club you belong to?"

"Why didn't I think of that myself?" said Harvey. "Would you happen to have an official Megalo Triplicate Copy Pad handy?"

Mr. Brisbane handed him the pad and Harvey proceeded to write out his resignation. He tore off the top copy and handed it to Mr. Brisbane.

Mr. Brisbane read the sheet. "Now, Harvey," he said, "sometimes your misplaced sense of humor carries you a bit far. I shall tear this up and then we'll both forget that this little incident ever occurred."

"What about the personnel office?" said Harvey. "Will they forget the copy I send them?"

"I think you are serious," said Mr. Brisbane.

Harvey was serious. The next day he bid farewell to Mr. Brisbane and the Megalo staff and moved his center of operations to the Garden Acres Indoor Tennis Club. There he spent his days, watching the matches, helping the manager with the tennis shop and playing whenever possible.

Harvey's wife Margaret took it all rather badly. The evening that he announced his resignation and his future plans they had a long whispered quarrel in the kitchen. Harvey had always wished that he could occasionally shout when they disagreed, but Margaret felt that it would be very bad for the children to be awakened by their parents' voices raised in anger.

"Why didn't you ask me before you resigned?" demanded Margaret. "That's what hurts the most. You didn't even consult your own wife."

"But I did," said Harvey. "I've been saying right along just how tired I was of coordinating research and how I thought I'd quit and do something I really liked. And you always smiled and told me how great you thought that would be."

"But I thought you meant another job," said Margaret.

"I guess I didn't mean that at all," said Harvey.

They sat in silence for several minutes. Then Margaret said, "Have you thought about the money? How are we going to live?"

"We'll have to use the savings," said Harvey. "That should keep us going for a while."

"But that money's for college for the children," said Margaret.

"I've decided that the kids don't need to go to college to be good tennis players," said Harvey. "Now I'll admit that most of the really good players in this country are college graduates, but I suspect that studying was really mostly a hindrance to them. If they could have put in all of their time working out on the courts, they would have been even better players." He stopped because his wife was crying.

"You're mad," she sobbed. "You've gone out of your mind."

The quarrel dragged on for another hour with no resolution. Margaret finally locked herself in the master bedroom and Harvey spent the night on the living room couch.

Their disagreement had shaken him up, Harvey realized when he missed a couple of easy overhead smashes in the first set he played the next day. But his game steadied after a couple of hours, and by the end of the afternoon he had forgotten that there had been any rupture in his domestic life.

It was thus with considerable shock that he discovered, on his return home that evening, that his packed suitcase was sitting on the front porch with a curt note from Margaret informing him that he would have to choose between marriage and indoor tennis. The very suddenness of this ultimatum caused Harvey to waver momentarily in his resolve. As he opened the suitcase to make sure that Margaret had packed all of his tennis socks, he thought for a moment of surrender to the comforts of hearth and home. But the socks, were all there, and he remembered with a warm glow of satisfaction how all of the kinks had come out of his backhand stroke in just two days of steady play. He put the suitcase in the car and drove over to West Street where he rented a furnished room two blocks from the tennis club.

When she heard her husband drive away, Margaret knew that it was time to get some professional advice. The next morning she dropped by the office of her good friend, Professor Helen Ralish. Helen was a professor of Social Dynamics at nearby Hartwell College and the author of *Marriage at the Bargaining Table*, the definitive work on marital negotiation.

"I wish you had called me before you escalated the situation," she said when Margaret had briefed her. "I'm afraid that putting him out of the house was at least a Level III threat."

"I could tell him I didn't mean it," said Margaret.

"Certainly not," said Helen. "Above all, we must maintain his belief in the viability of your threats. To back down at this stage of negotiations would destroy all credibility in your future actions."

"What should I do then?" asked Margaret.

"The initial step in any bargaining process is evaluation. We must delineate the goals of each party and then list a series of threats, in order of magnitude, that you are willing to bring against your opponent."

"But he's not my opponent, he's my husband," said Margaret.

"Certainly," said Helen, "but for the sake of your marriage you must try to view the situation in terms of a simple bargaining model. Now what do you suppose are his goals?"

"I guess he wants to play tennis for the rest of his life," said Margaret with a sigh.

"Which is unsatisfactory from your point of view," said Helen. "What would be a goal acceptable to you that would allow your husband to feel that he had come out somewhat ahead at the bargaining table?"

"I guess he'd be happier if he could return to doing research instead of management," said Margaret.

"You must make sure that Harvey understands that this is an achievable goal," said Helen.

"He knows they want him back," said Margaret.

"Now for the threats," said Helen. "Is Harvey very religious?"

"We go to church almost every Sunday," said Margaret.

"We'll put that down as a Level I threat," said Helen. "Ostracism by the religious community."

"But I don't think that Reverend Plackley would put him out of the church just for playing tennis," said Margaret.

"I am not talking of the church in the sense of an 18th century religious entity," said Helen. "I am speaking here of the social alienation of Harvey by his peers in the church socio-religious group. Now what other of his peers would be willing to bring pressure directly on him?"

"There's Mel Winters at the bank," said Margaret. "Harvey respects him a great deal."

"Good," said Helen. "Anyone else?"

Margaret could think of no one else. "That will have to do then," said Helen. "I'll take care of briefing Reverend Plackley."

The Rev. Raymond Plackley was distressed when he heard of the situation in the Wellfleet household and agreed that pressure from the church community might well be the lever by which Harvey could be pried back to reason.

The Rev. Plackley felt that he should bring aid and comfort directly to his flock in the fields. He had achieved much renown by giving a series of morning Bible readings in beauty salons, and his Book of the Psalms, translated into the vernacular of truck drivers, had won a prominent place on the book stands on the wayside restaurants of America. It was thus with complete comfort that he removed his clerical garments and dressed in tennis whites in the locker room of the tennis club. The ostensible reason for his visit was to work on his game under Harvey's tutelage. However, at the proper moment, he intended to impart to Harvey the extreme concern that the members of the church felt over his irresponsible behavior.

It took Harvey only a few minutes to determine the faults in Plackley's game. He called him up to the net. "Ray," he said, "there are three things wrong with your tennis. You don't keep your eyes on the ball, you crowd your forehand and you need a lot of practice. Now, to begin with, concentrate on watching the ball. I shall shout at you when you crowd your forehand."

The changes in the minister's game were immediate and spectacular. His forehand stroke, long a quietly endured agony of awkwardness, suddenly became a thing of beauty. He felt his whole body moving with a rhythm never before experienced. It was, as he explained in the locker room afterward, almost a religious experience. He was overjoyed and could not thank Harvey enough for his assistance.

The telephone rang a few minutes after the Rev. Plackley had returned to the rectory. It was Helen

Ralish. "I just wanted to check with you," she said, "on Mr. Wellfleet's reaction to what you told him."

"As a matter of fact," said Plackley, "we never got around to discussing that problem. I felt it would be best if he brought the matter up himself." He switched the receiver to his left hand, picked up his racquet from the hall table and made a couple of furtive swings to make sure that the beauty of motion still dwelt within him.

"You're saying you didn't tell him," said Helen.

"I'm sure I'll have the opportunity soon," said the minister. "I've made arrangements to play with Harvey once a week from now on."

"No, thanks," said Helen. "I don't think it would do much good."

She hung up and turned to Margaret, who was sitting in her office. "I think the reverend has surrendered to the pleasures of the flesh," she said. "I hope this banker friend of yours is made of sterner stuff."

Mel Winters was of tougher fiber. When Helen explained the situation to him, he agreed to the plan in its entirety. "I've been worried about Harvey myself," he said, "both from the personal and professional standpoints. A man without a job can't keep up his mortgage payments very long. Now I feel that a very strong approach is in order here. I'll go down, whip him soundly in a couple of sets and then lay it on the line to him."

Mel had never had any problem in the past in whipping Harvey at singles. He always won in straight sets. Mel hit the ball hard and with precision, a reflection of the way of life that had made him a respected vice-president of the Garden Acres National Bank.

However, he discovered that constant practice had significantly improved Harvey's game. Mel's hard, deep drives came back across the net just as hard and just as deep. Nevertheless, he felt that it was due to some very lucky shots on Harvey's part that Harvey won the first set 6-4. His loss to Harvey in the second set by 6-2 was a lot more disturbing.

It was still necessary that he inform Harvey of his ostracism. Mel sat Harvey down in the lounge and carefully explained his reasons. "You understand," he concluded, "that this gives me a great deal of pain. I have valued our friendship a great deal and look forward to it continuing when you resume your role of responsibility in the community."

Harvey broke into laughter. "I never thought I'd see the day you'd be a bad sport," he said.

"What do you mean, bad sport!" demanded Mel.

"Today was the first time I ever took a set from you," said Harvey. "And as soon as we walk off the court you trump up this wild story about my responsibilities to the community. You're afraid to play me, that's the whole of it. You know I can slaughter you any time I feel like it."

With a great mental effort Mel suppressed his anger. "You must believe me," he said. "I had decided to say what I just told you long before we ever walked out onto that tennis court."

"Sure," said Harvey. "You lay awake all night making this tough decision. Come off it, Mel. Admit you're nothing but a plain old-fashioned bad loser."

It was useless to argue with Harvey, Mel picked up his racquet, his clothes and what was left of his dignity and walked out of the club with Harvey's laughter echoing in his ears.

The next day Helen held a grim conference with Margaret in her office. "Your husband has turned out to be a clever opponent," she said. "He has managed to convince us of his incredulity in all of the threats we have made. I can see no other alternative than an immediate escalation to Level IV. You must serve him with divorce papers."

"I can't bring myself to do that," said Margaret.

There was one other source of help. Margaret called her sister Josh.

Josh, her husband George and their 16-year-old son Milton drove over the next Saturday from their home in nearby Brentwood. Milton immediately borrowed his father's car and disappeared. As Margaret had sent her children to a movie, the adults were left alone to talk. They looked at the problem from every angle but could find no solution.

After nearly two hours Milton returned. Milton was short and plump, wore black-rimmed glasses and walked as if each step gave him violent pains in his arches. He dropped into a chair and propped his feet up on the coffee table. "I understand Uncle Harvey's been giving you trouble," he said.

"That is none of your business," said his mother. "We are having a family discussion, and I think it would be better if you left."

"O.K.," said Milton with a wave of his fat hand. "I've figured out a solution to the problem, but if you're not interested , forget it."

He started to rise, but Margaret said to Josh, "Milton is a member of the family, and I think his suggestion should carry some weight." She tried to keep the desperation out of her voice.

Milton smiled and slouched back into his chair. "I was over at the tennis club this morning checking out Uncle Harvey," she said.

"You didn't play tennis with him, did you?" said Margaret.

"Of course not. I am not a mesomorph who must continually run around flexing his muscles to prove they'll flex. As an activator, I observe, cogitate and then plan the actions of others."

"Milton," said his father, "if you have a suggestion to make, please make it."

"I am trying to explain," said Milton. "I have observed Uncle Harvey and his tennis game. I have thought over the problem. I have a solution."

"So tell us," said Josh.

"I have a solution," said Milton, "and now I would like to state my price."

"Milton," said his father, "if you think for a minute you can pull another of your blackmail schemes, you are wrong. I told you the television set was the last of such bribes."

Milton smiled placidly at his parents. "We have discussed the matter of my mobility before, I think," he said.

"You are not going to have a car, and that is final," shouted his father.

"And," continued Milton, "I think I presented a rather reasonaable compromise. All I require, you may remember, is transportation. I am not one who takes delight in the styling of power available in a motor vehicle. But I do dislike walking when an inexpensive alternative is available."

"We should have known better," said Josh.

There was a long silence. Finally George said, "I know it's hopeless to appeal to your better nature or your sense of fair play. How much do you want?"

"Let us say $300 for the vehicle and at least half the insurance premiums," said Milton.

"He doesn't get this streak from my side of the family," said his father. "O.K., it's a deal, but only if your solution actually works."

"Of course," said Milton. "Now to get down to essentials. Who would you say is the worst tennis player in the Garden Acres Indoor Tennis Club? Is there perhaps someone whose game Uncle Harvey derides?"

"Leland Harwich," said Margaret without hesitation. "That would be 'Flub Shot' Harwich."

"Fine," said Milton. "My plan is simplicity itself. I shall train Mr. Harwich to whip Uncle Harvey. It should not be difficult. Uncle Harvey strokes the ball well, but he does not play intelligently and he does not react well to pressure. In most sports the man who uses his head can usually defeat a better-coordinated player who does not think on the court."

Leland Harwich agreed to go along with Milton's plan, as he would have with any scheme that might eliminate the term Flub Shot from general usage at the tennis club. To cover for his absence from the club, Milton had Leland's arm fitted with a removable cast, and the story circulated that it had been broken in a fall in his bathtub. Four times a week Leland drove to the Brentwood Indoor Tennis Center where he removed his cast and worked out with the pro under Milton's supervision. Milton concentrated upon building Leland's confidence in a few simple strokes and gave him long lectures on his uncle's weaknesses. In less than three months Milton gave the go-ahead for the final phase of his plan.

Leland threw away his cast and appeared one-morning at the Garden Acres Club. Harvey was sitting, feet up, in the lounge watching a doubles match on the near court. "How's the arm?" he said when he saw Leland.

"Fine," said Leland. "Been out of the cast for a week. All set to give it a little exercise."

It was Harvey's natural reaction to offer to hit a few balls with Leland. After they had been banging the ball for about 15 minutes, Leland stopped and called to Harvey. "The arm feels so good I'd like to play a few games until I feel it tightening up."

"Sure thing," shouted Harvey. "Serve them up!"

The first serve came at Harvey with a high deceptive bounce. He swung desperately at it and drove it up into the rafters under the club roof. Harvey inspected the grip of his racquet. His hand must have slipped. No one ever had trouble returning Flub Shot's serve.

But the tricky serves continued. The game went to Leland, and it was Harvey's service. Now the real horror began. Leland returned Harvey's service effortlessly, driving him back and forth across the court with tireless ease. The kink suddenly reappeared in Harvey's backhand, and his forehand shots developed a strange propensity for the bottom of the net. He felt all of his hard-won coordination rapidly slipping away.

Leland won the first set 6-1. Harvey demanded a second set although Leland complained of a slight soreness in his arm. Now anger completed the degradation of Harvey's game. His smooth swing degenerated into a little Ping-Pong chop that dropped lazily in front of Leland. All timing disappeared from Harvey's serve.

When Leland carefully placed the final shot just out of Harvey's reach to win the set 6-0, Harvey's wrath exploded. "This idiot game!" he shouted. "I work forever building up my game, and some punk comes along and pushes me all over the court. I am through! Never again will I play this stupidity!" He hammered his racquet against one of the steel uprights until it was reduced to a tangle of gut and splinters.

There is little more to Harvey's story. Still true to

his vow, he has taken up golf as an occasional weekend relaxation from his work in the Megalo research laboratory. His nephew drives a 5-year-old Mercury with an insolence that is only just tolerated by his parents.

Life in the Wellfleet household is almost back to normal, but throughout Garden Acres there is a new uneasiness in the air. Wherever housewives gather, in coffee klatch of supermarket aisle, worried whispers may be heard—"I think my husband was only kidding, but he talked for an hour last night about the beautiful deal that Harvey Wellfleet had for himself."

"That's nothing. Burton keeps talking about Harvey's one mistake. He keeps saying that when he becomes a tennis bum, nothing at all will ever get him back to work."

What the future holds for Garden Acres is difficult to say. John Petland, the manager of the tennis club, is optimistic. "Business was never better," he often says. "The men of this community are realizing more and more that there is considerably more to life than just the grind at the office. Each of us needs a certain amount of relaxation and recreation in his life." And then he smiles, as if only he knows just how large that amount might be.

"Watch your body language . . . they'll think you're tired."

"Beautiful job of first-aid."

More Than You Ever Wanted to Know about Your Racquet

CAROL KLEIMAN

Choosing a new tennis racquet—or being chosen by one—can be as traumatic an event as picking a college, selecting a mate, or being pregnant.

Recently, I announced to the world that I was in a condition of needing a new tennis racquet, and I have been inundated ever since with the best of advice, concern, warning, fears, sympathy and favorite stories.

I have been playing tennis full time—that means the time since I have not let anything inconsequential such as job or family interfere with my sport—for almost six years.

I never had trouble picking a racquet before because I didn't know very much about tennis. Now, a little knowledge has become a dangerous thing.

My first racquet, naturally, was a light wooden one, easy to hold, had been in the family for years, and everyone recommended it. For one year I played with it, inexpensive nylon string and all. Actually, I finally needed a new one because I had worn out the frame— the nylon was in *perfect* shape.

It was followed by an equally traditional wood, one step up in size and power, a medium, 4½. It felt so heavy I could barely hold it, but I lusted after it because some women whom I then considered good players used it.

My game remained at the same level, very low. I used two hands to bring the racquet back, both forehand and backhand. I never adjusted to it and vice versa.

Then, a marvelous friend rescued me. He is a doctor, and he encouraged another doctor to give up tennis because both agreed the latter's game was too terrible to continue. When the second doctor flung his steel racquet for the final time, my friend caught it and gave it to me. And that's how I got to win a 4½ medium, strung with gut, steel racquet.

Immediately—after what I had been through it is no wonder—my game picked up. Suddenly, I had pace and timing and style and my elbow did not severely ache. The steel racquet did marvelous things at the net, all by itself, that I could have never done at all. That racquet never left my side for four years. It went with me on vacations, to tournaments, to local clubs.

Then last summer, during a two-week marathon tennis trip to Sleepy Hollow Resort in South Haven, Mich., my steelie had a nervous breakdown, right on the court. It crunched in half after a particularly disastrous backhand.

As soon as proper sympathy was expressed for my loss, old tennis racquet tales began volleying in from all over the court.

"Here's a chance to improve your groundstrokes. Get a wooden racquet and start really playing tennis."

"Don't buy an aluminum racquet unless you always hit in the center of the racquet. Otherwise, the strings break." Then, after watching me hit with one, "Don't buy an aluminum racquet."

"Get a steel. Otherwise, you'll ruin your elbow."

"Only tournament players who are paid to play with steel ever play with steel. The best racquet is wood."

"Don't buy a heavy wood racquet. It feels like a club."

"There's nothing like the aluminum racquets. They are super."

"Steel is perfected now. It helps your game enormously."

"Fiberglass is fantastic."

Everyone lent me his or her racquet and watched anxiously, seeing if I approved or not. For one week, I borrowed this one and that one, feeling alone, afraid, and insecure without my own security racquet.

Finally, I made my decision: I bought a wooden racquet, the stiffest one of all—the club, remember? If steel and wood are put on a scale of one to 10 for flexibility, my steel racquet was one and my new wooden one is 10.

Why? I want to improve my groundstrokes and serve. I miss those old wood shots of mine; I know I'll be able to get them back again with just a little practice. Besides, the pro at Sleepy Hollow offered me *his* new and strung, for only $20.

And you should see how *he* hits the ball!

"Harold..."

"About this tennis you're playing on your lunch hour..."

"Well, after 20 years of trying, say hello to the club champ, Agnes."

"Hey, that's cheating!"

The Camels-and-Gypsies Circuit

JOHN
TULLIUS

It's a sunny, breezy day on the Costa del Sol of southern Spain and Terry Hayes, an itinerant former college player from Cincinnati, is lounging by the courts at the Malaga Tennis Club, sipping wine and telling stories to a pack of tennis gypsies like himself. They're players who, for the most part, have found the big-money international circuits a bit too hectic, too vicious. Instead, they float around among the dozens of European circuits, tournaments and pick-up events which offer the full gamut of competition and prize money.

Once you've been there a while, you get to know the ropes. There are little local village wee-wows where, if you need a hundred bad, you can smoke your way into the finals. Or you can get into the qualifiers at the French or the Italian Opens and, maybe, get a shot at Borg. Heaven forbid! Most of these gypsies prefer to follow the middle ground—the small circuits which are run in each country and which, if you're savvy enough, can feed you year round.

In Malaga, Hayes has gotten into the 16's, which means he's guaranteed $85. So he's feeling good; $85 in Spain will get you room, board, drunk and disco'd for three weeks. And when Hayes is feeling good, he talks.

"I'd just played a tournament in Greece," he begins, "and kicked some pretty good talent. Got to the quarters and I was feeling ebullient. The next tournament was in the Middle East a week off and I thought I'd try to fulfill one of my lifetime ambitions—to ride a horse across the Turkish-Persian plains like Alex the Great. So I buy this fiery steed in Istanbul—one of those gray models with the white sidewalls like Tonto used to ride. To celebrate, I stay up all night partying at the Puddin Shoppe and listening to horror stories from all the broke American kids who got hepatitis swimming in the Ganges. Man, what your guru don't tell you!"

"So next day I pack up Trojan, my horse, and pretty soon I'm out there on the Kush with a horse full of racquets. And I camp out the first night and I'm out there in the beautiful all alone, just me and 10,000 nomads who'd cut your gizzards out for your shoes.

"Next day I wake up and after about two hours of a nice leisurely pace, Trojan slows to a saunter, then a walk and then just stops. Dead. Head down. In the middle of the desert. Nothin'. I look around for snakes or water or some reason for my trusty mount to stop. Nothin'. We're miles and miles from nothin'. Not a road. Not a shack. Not a tent. Nothin'. Then his knees buckle and his eyes roll up in his head and thump! He falls over on his side and he's stone dead before he hits the ground. With me in a heap on top of him still half in the saddle. I got to work for an hour just to get my racquets out from underneath his carcass.

"Then I set out on foot. And man I'm scared. I'm not worried about surviving or anything like that. I'm worried cause I got to make it to the next tournament on time. See, it's part of a seven-event tour and if you miss one tournament the sponsors drop you. I gotta get there and I got five days to do it. So it takes me a day of hoofin' it to reach a tiny little village on the main highway and it's me and 50 Bulgarians trying to get a ride from the one car that comes through every three hours.

"The only thing I got to eat is some bee pollen I picked up in Spain. Unless, of course, I wanna buy a bowl of 10-day-old rice heated on a fire made from goat droppings—which I don't. But you know what? The only thing that was really bothering me was my backhand was a little shaky in the last tournament."

An Australian mate, Jimmy Devlin, burps out: "That's no backhand. It's a bloody folding chair." Which draws lots of crude hee-haws. Hayes nods his head in agreement and doesn't miss a beat.

"So, of course, I got out my racquet and start to hit balls against a wall. It's really a glorious day and I really start getting into it—whacking overheads and playing points out. Just when I pass Connors to win the first set 7-5, this Mercedes roars by and slams on the brakes and skids about 500 feet and does a complete doughnut. Then it backs up to where I'm at and there's this beautiful French woman inside and she rolls down her window and sticks her head out and says: 'Want a ride?'"

"I won't bore you with the romantic details..."

"Why not? It won't take but a minute." That's Devlin again.

"But when I pull into the tournament in this new silver 300 SL with a gorgeous French woman, all the players' mouths fell to their belts and finally someone yells out, 'Hey, Hayes! I thought you were gonna ride here on a frickin' horse?' And I give the side of the car a loud slap and yell back. 'Yep! 400 ponies right here.' YAAAHAAAA! They liked that one."

Hayes and his fellow gypsies are essentially adventurers—free-spirited, outrageous characters who eventually drift through tennis circles everywhere and spice up the game with their colorful, often hilarious, subculture.

In Europe, they start out in the spring in Belgium and France, then move on to Germany and Italy in the summer, and Spain and the French Riviera in the fall and early winter. From here, it's Istanbul, Athens, Beirut...

By far the most attractive tournaments, from the standpoint of prize money, hospitality and competition, are on the Spanish circuit. (It's not really a circuit but a bunch of separately run tournaments at places like San Sebastian, Granada and La Gorilla—rated on a scale from one to five. The prize money in the top tournaments runs around $5,000. It drops off at the lesser events and, in fact, the tournaments at the bottom of the scale are usually nothing more than social affairs with all proceeds going to the local padre to re-upholster the pews.

Of course, if a player does well enough in these local events, he can pick up a handful of computer points and eventually work his way into the pre-qualifying and qualifying rounds at the Grand Prix events in places like Barcelona and Madrid. But as Hayes puts it: "You play Manuel Orantes every week, you starve. Most of us ain't looking to build a big tennis future. We wanna fool around in Europe, see the world, have a good time for as long as we can keep it going. We're on a five-year vacation. We don't want to be No. 1."

The majority of the real grubbers on these circuits are American or Australian, and the rest are mostly South Americans. Their common characteristic seems to be a quizzical look and a facility to wing it. Oh, there are plenty of other countries represented, but those players hardly qualify as gypsies. There's a group of western Europeans but, let's face it, they're home really. And a vagabond at home is a solid citizen. They can be under daddy's roof in a couple hours of thumbing or call for money and collect that same day.

And those guys from Rumania, Czechoslovakia and Bulgaria are all on expense accounts. That's right —expense accounts! Not exactly a fortune, but enough for air fare, hotels and all they can eat. I mean, it isn't what Nastase or Ruzici pull down, but on these circuits, it'll do.

And even among the Americans, a good 75 percent come over for only a couple of months, have a certain amount of money saved up from trying to teach senior citizens to hit backhands and they go until they run out of coins and hop on a homeward-bound Freddy Laker. You can always spot this American brat bunch. They all hang out together and they all wear the uniform— designer duds, Adidas warm-ups, Hang Ten socks and their junior rankings.

When you think about it, though, they are probably the smartest of the bunch. they have a tennis vacation with a round-trip ticket, hotel rooms, rent-a-heap and all. The smartest, yes, but not the most spirited. They are not the heartbeat of these circuits. They fly here and back to their cushy assistant pro jobs at one of those Beach 'n Tennis spas so fast it'd make your Jacuzzi spin.

Of the true tennis gypsies, there are two types.

First, there are those who come on one-way tickets and trip over their shoestring budgets pretty quickly. They start out in the French Riviera or Italy or Austria when they should have stayed in Spain where you can still get by on a dollar a day if you have to. So they end up under their vans, climbing in hotel windows after lock-up, sleeping on the club courts or in the locker room—living on French bread, bad water and glucose pills.

There are a lot of anxious moments on these last-ditch circuits. The TV smart alecks are always talking about the pressure of playing for $100,000. But how about the pressure of a guy who's halfway around the world and he's serving at 30-40, down 4-5 in the third and he's got to win this match or he may never see mom and dad and sis again. This match is his escape. It's his Midnight Express. It's like Lee Trevino said: "Pressure is when you've got $20 on a putt and you've only got $10 in your pocket."

The second group of tennis gypsies, the ones who stay a while, operate like small businessmen. They stay at the two-star hotels or pensions; that is, when they can't find the hotel that'll take 10 guys to a room and feed them all breakfast for the same price. And when the body aches or they have lost a flub-dubber or gotten a case of the rampant "turistas" (and for a while play cannot be continuous), then they stay at a four-star-hot-shower-maid-service-screened-in paradise for three times what it's worth but at that moment is price-less to their spent body and mind.

The most important thing is the maid, which might sound pretty spoiled. But think about this: each player has at least two matches a day and, even if he loses, with doubles and consolation rounds everyone is usually very busy. On European clay, the abrasion of sliding can create severe blistering on the feet. So everyone wears at least three pairs of socks, or six pairs a day. Twelve socks times seven days is 84 socks a week. And they're not just smelly, they're thickly caked with red clay from toe to ankle. Add sweat and let it harden and you've got more than dirty socks; you've got a piece of avant-garde pottery.

You have to scrub all night over a sink to try to get the clay out so you have some semblance of a white sock. And if you think there's a laundromat in the whole of Spain or the French Riviera, then you've been living in Rolling Hills Estates too long—which is exactly what most of these kids have been doing.

If you wake up one morning and you're out of socks, you have to play in soggy just-washed ones. It happens all the time to spoiled types who've never washed a plate, much less done their own laundry. And it gets to them. It grinds at their pride and their faltering psyches and gnaws their pampered egos into mush. You can always tell these guys—they're the ones with the squishy sneakers!

There are other tricks the players pick up to survive. There is, for example, the constant selling of equipment. It's the old traveler's game of buy cheap here, sell high there. Often enough you'll see a player who had 20 racquets when he arrived, down to two in short order. Also, the players will often string racquets, give lessons or hit with the tournament director's son, which somehow seems to be its own reward. It all helps.

But what helps the most, by far, is learning how to play on that infernal red clay. How long can a man buoy his spirit when he's run into the ground week after week by guys with poopy serves and marshmallow strokes? To play a guy who'd be just another hacker at your club back home, to work like a sled dog for five hours and to barely eke out a victory, well, it gets to you. Finally you say, "Who needs it? I don't want to be out here anymore." And that's why you see a lot of scores in Europe like 7-6, 6-0. The guy tanked it; just couldn't hang in there.

The hard thing on clay is to establish the frame of mind that you're going to be there a while. There's a joke in Europe. You take your lunch to the courts. Or your dinner. Or your lunch and dinner. It's hard for a fast-living American or Australian (who's used to getting the match over in an hour) to accept the fact that the first set probably won't end in an hour.

Many Americans have never played five straight

hours (have you?), never experienced the pain of
cramps. Five long, gruelling, frustrating hours! How
long can the spirit hold out in a kid who came over with
expensive strokes, Fila shorts and a Roscoe Tanner
perm? How long will he hold out on that court against a
maniac ball retriever who'll do anything to get the ball
back—push it, kick it, fall on his face? For what? For 20
bucks! You must be kidding!

Europe, they soon find out, is a different world.
But for those who can adapt, like Hayes and Devlin, it's
a good life. The two of them tour around in an old
Austin minibus that they picked up in Scotland. It has a
motor that sounds like a soup-spoon riot at a prison.
But they know where the action is, on and off the court,
and it gets them there.

One night after play is finished at Malaga, for example, they head for a night of rascality at a dive called
the "Elephante Discoteca." When the music plays, bits
of plaster fall off the walls and ceiling. The drinks are
served in glasses with old lipstick smudges, the bar-
tenders shortchange you like it's their right and the
place smells like a YMCA. But there are girls. Are there
ever girls!

Hayes has pulled off a table coup d'etat and the
bunch of us are ensconced in a huge table right off the
dance floor and between dances Hayes shouts in my
ear:

"The old style tennis bum was just a tourist. But
most of us live here. You've got to or you couldn't make
it. You've got to know every cheap hotel and restau-
rant. And not the sleaze bags, either, or you'd go nuts.
You wouldn't be able to keep it together and have fun.
And fun is what this whole thing's about.

"A lot of kids come over here and they're good
players. But they can't stay long. You gotta know every
angle. Like there's this little tournament on Corsica
that Jimmy and I always go to and the rest of them
think we're balmy in the crumpets. But, see, they always have this snooker tournament at a hotel in town,
and even though we get nothin' for three days of
tennis, we clean up at the snooker table. Or when we go

to Greece, we always take a fishin' boat over to the islands because they got these resorts with Arab billionaires and they ain't got nobody to play with. So you can make 20, 30 bucks an hour hittin' with them. Made $400 between us one year."

Hayes points out to the dance floor and there's Devlin dancing away with no one in particular—wild-eyed, head dipped back, just dancing.

"This is a special breed," Hayes continues. "they talk about the early barnstormers as adventurous, but there ain't nobody like these guys. Of anybody making money in tennis, these guys are the farthest out on the limb. The only reason they can make it is because of all the money in tennis now. Why, even park tournaments in places like Wash Tub, Washington, have a little money in 'em now. It's a phenomenon. We're a phenomenon. But all this exaggerated prize money will end. It's gotta end. And that's when this breed will end."

Murderous Pleasures of the Game

NAT HENTOFF

We tennis zealots are growing in numbers.

In more and more summer communities, tennis schedules, especially on weekends, are so tightly packed that a newcomer finds himself scheduled either at a time that gets him up before his children or so late in the day that he needs the sharpness of eye of an Indian scout.

Why has slamming a ball with a racquet become so obsessive a pleasure for so many of us?

It seems clear to me that a primary attraction of the sport is the opportunity it gives to release aggression physically without being arrested for felonious assault.

Consider the tensions and frustrations increasingly endemic to our tautly rationalized society. And then consider the entirely legal stance of mayhem permissible on a tennis court. As Dr. Roy M. Whitman, associate professor of psychiatry at the University of Cincinnati, has pointed out, there is an element of homicide, although unconscious, in the game. There are, to be sure, the exemplary manners. ("Thank you, Court 3," you call, your ball whizzing into Court 3 just as one of its players is about to serve. And Court 3 nods benignly and returns the ball.) But alongside the exemplary manners, the doctor notes, is the brutal volleying climax.

Hyperbole? Look at the faces of lawyers, accountants, admen, psychiatrists, housewives, and poets immersed in a set. Particularly during a doubles match, look at the faces of the guardians of the net. Nancy Richey, a top-ranked American player, has observed, with some awe at her capacity for ferociousness, "When I see a picture of myself playing, even I'm frightened."

There are few more satisfying experiences, I find,

than putting a ball away with all one's force. Even more satisfying is a duel at the net, each of us flailing away like a medieval knight with mace or broadsword. And invariably, of course, the loser of a particular exchange pulls himself back into civilization with a "Good shot!" or "Well played!" or, more honestly, "Too good!"

It is hardly any wonder, then, that tennis is booming in as aggressive, and aggressively competitive, a society as ours. But, alas, with some players, as in life outside the courts, the competitiveness often constricts and distorts the gloriously full release of aggression. From the first years of school on, we are taught, on the one hand, that competitiveness is both a virtue and a necessity. How else can we move up to consume all those delectable goods? How else can we win and maintain the respect of our wives and children?

But on the other hand, there are manners to be observed, styles of behavior, tones of voice. One should not be too "pushy," too "cocky," too "loud." In short, too overtly aggressive. The cool, poised, soft-spoken expert at lethal competitiveness is a figure of respect by contrast with the noisy tie salesman on the street corner.

And so, on the tennis courts, there are those who are so acutely conscious of their need to WIN that they tighten up in fear that they will not win as gentlemen. They find it painfully difficult to sustain the savage drive which winning requires, and if they're in a doubles match, they then feel they have let down their partner. He, after all, also wants fiercely to WIN. Therefore, there is the grim shaking of the head, the turning to the partner after you have muffed an easy point, the mournful "I'm sorry!", the jaw-set determination to make up for the error. And the partner, smiling, is reassuring: "No, that was a tough shot." Or, "The wind took it." Thinking, meanwhile, "Why did I have to get stuck with him?"

A few players are so obsessed with winning, and so ambivalent about the drive it takes to win, that tennis is a torture for them. One such masochist arrives on the court with a sheaf of excuses. A bad elbow. A distract-

ingly complicated business day. A sudden discovery
that he needs a lighter racquet. He girds himself to
overcome these obstacles and fulfill his responsibility
to his partner; and by the end of an hour, he is quiver-
ing, drenched in the chill sweat of failure.

Occasionally, there is a further dimension of competitive urgency in tennis. For many years, the sport
was largely a game for white Protestants. Gradually,
more and more Jews of the middle class took it up. I
play most often, for example, with Jewish professionals
in their thirties and forties to whose fathers the game
of tennis was as exotic as croquet.

Most of the time, we hardly think of the game's
social and class origins. But for a few days in the summer we do. Our community on Fire Island is called
Seaview. It began as a restricted Protestant enclave,
and while it is now mostly Jewish, still among us is that
patriarchal first Jew who dared buy property in Seaview. Two communities away is Point O' Woods, which
still does not admit Jews, let alone Negroes. For the
past few summers, there has been a home-and-home
series between Seaview and Point O' Woods. Our Mac-
cabees venture forth for a day through the Point O'
Woods gate, and some weeks later, a contingent of
doughty WASP's come unto us.

One of our very best players refuses to compete in
these ecumencial engagements. His contention, which
I respect, is that so long as he is unable to lease property
in Point O' Woods because he is Jewish, any other
contact between the two communities is hypocritical
and demeaning. Most of our players, however, act like
old-time Negroes, feeling that sport and social contact
will eventually convince the elders of Point O' Woods
to remove their gate. At least figuratively.

The gate remains, and the series goes on. We lose
more often than we win, and one of the reasons appears to be that some of our champions go on the court
burdened by history. Watching them, I think of how
Joe Louis must have felt.

Last summer, the Point O' Woods team came to
Seaview in the middle of a community debate about

whether we would accede to Point O' Woods' request to share our new garbage incinerator with them. Seaview was virulently divided on the issue, but nonetheless a cross section of the residents came to watch the joust. Curiosity is a major factor in drawing even non-tennis-players to the event. For many of us, our ghettos are much more comfortable than those of the parents, but ghettos they are. Accordingly, we do not often see Protestants at play. The summer before, for instance, my son and I were taken by an expletive frequently used by one of the more elderly Point O' Woods players. When he drove the ball into the net or served a double fault, he did not, as we Seaviewers do, growl "Damn!" or "Jesus Christ!" He would release a fierce "Golly Ned!" But how fierce can "Golly Ned!" be? And for a few months, my five-year-old, at times of extreme irritation, would also bellow "Golly Ned!" but the cross-culturation didn't take.

In any case, as our players warmed up, waiting for the WASP's, our intense captain, a very successful po-diatrist, looked coldly at our most aggressive player, a short redhead on whom we placed most of our hopes for the day. "Say, Mel," the captain muttered, "Tuck your shirt in." At that moment, I knew we were lost. We were still of the *Shtetl,* and sabras we would never be.

Soon after the match started, we quickly fell be-hind. Some of our players tried to keep up their spirits, and ours, with ghetto wit. "If they win," Mel whispered to me during a break, "they get to use our incinerator for three days—on us."

The playing on our side was pitiful, for the most part. Men whose grace, control, and stamina I had long envied played as if millions of Jews were watching them, at first hopefully and then with accusatory con-tempt. And Mel, our most reckless, our most self-con-fident player, who always made impossible recoveries, played with such caution, such defensiveness, that he and his partner were defeated by an older and quite ordinary team.

It was a dun Saturday. But perhaps, an onlooker ventured, we had been overwhelmed *because* we were playing on Saturday. Mel brightened a bit. "Yeah, next year we'll play on *their* Sabbath, and then we'll see what happens."

There is, to be sure, as psychiatrist Roy Whitman declares, more than a touch of homicide in tennis, but there is also a quickening of life in the pursuit and pleasure of the game. Certainly more kinetic life than I had thought myself still capable of. I'm too old for LSD, and I wonder what would have become of me had it not been for tennis. Tim Leary has his religion, and now I have mine. Tennis Power! Better health through

"Okay, on the next stroke, please stand farther apart..."

murder. And the corpses can so easily be replaced in cans of three.

Soon my sons will be old enough to start to learn. A Hentoff at Forest Hills! At Wimbledon! Vicarious Tennis Power! But, Dr. Whitman warns, those tennis players who are taught by their fathers achieve a sense of murderous satisfaction by decisively defeating the old boys once they have surpassed their fathers' ability. This will come as no surprise to me. I have read *The Golden Bough*. But grant me life at least until my sons play Point O' Woods.

Maybe We Belong on the Golf Course

SYDNEY J.
HARRIS

Matthew Arnold once famously declared that every person in the world was either a Platonist or an Aristotelian—whether or not he knows it, or has even heard of these lofty terms.

Crudely translated from the academic, he meant that everyone belongs to one of two basic and opposite types of personality: the Platonic, which values the abstract realm of pure ideas; or the Aristotelian, which respects the senses and the realm of experience.

On a less elevated plane, W. S. Gilbert, in his comic opera, "Iolanthe," rhymingly asserted that: 'Every little boy and girl/Who comes into this world alive/Is either a little liberal/Or else a little conservative."

In much the same dogmatic way, I have through the years come to divide people into "tennis players" and "golfers." This applies not only to those who play these games, buy even to those who play no games at all. (Indeed, in my view, there are golfers who are tennis players at heart and tennis players who belong on the fairway, instead.)

Perhaps the most nearly perfect protoypes of these divergent personalities in American life were Dwight D. Eisenhower and Adlai E. Stevenson, who twice opposed each other as candidates for the Presidency. Eisenhower, of course, won handily—not primarily because he was a statesman, or even a general, but because he was a golfer. And the golfer type in the U.S. outnumbers the tennis type by at least 10 to 1.

What were the basic differences between Eisenhower and Stevenson? There were many—socially, intellectually, temperamentally, even morphologically (the body-build of the golfer tends to differ decisively from the body-build of the tennist.)

Eisenhower was bluff, practical, unimaginative, conventional, predictable, reliable, and perpetually boyish despite the "father image" he projected in politics. He never really outgrew his formative years, his addiction to cowboy films and escape reading, and died believing the same pioneer pieties he had been brought up never to question.

Stevenson, on the contrary, was more reserved, speculative, verbal, questioning, and far less locker-roomish. He did not exude raw masculinity (which doubtless injured his chances at the polls), and was painfully able to see both sides of any question—which earned him an unjustified reputation for "indecisiveness."

Obviously, not all golfers and tennists conform to these stereotypes. There are variations and combinations of personalities to be found in each group, shadings that move toward each other from both ends of the spectrum. But, generally speaking, there is more than an accidental faithfulness to the Eisenhower or Stevenson typology.

In his pure type, the tennist finds the golfer insufferably hearty; in his pure type, the golfer finds the tennist vaguely effete.

The golfer, on the whole, tends more to be a "man's man." He engages in lengthy and (to the tennist) boring autopsies of the game just played; the tennist, while more reflective about serious matters, rarely engages in postmortems of more than a sentence or two.

Some 40 years ago, Jean Giraudoux, the French playwright, observed: "The golf course is the epitome of all that is purely transitory in the universe, a space not to dwell in but to get over as quickly as possible."

That may be a somewhat unfair and extreme statement, but it is true that the golfer flees the course the moment the game is over, seemingly oblivious of its beauty or vernal ambiance. He hastens to the sanctuary of the "19th hole" where he can drink, swear, ruminate about his putting and swap dirty jokes.

The tennis player, however, lingers on the court, which is more of a "dwelling" than a "space" to him. He relishes the ambiance, enjoys watching others play and even finds the familiar hiss of a new can of balls being opened a lovely and evocative sound.

The antipodal nature of tennists and golfers even extends to politics where, it seems, the former tend to be more liberal and flexible, the latter more conservative and rigid. This is not to make the foolish assumption that there is any one-to-one correlation between game preferences and voting habits; obviously, there are many Republican tennists, and not a few Democratic golfers.

But it is to suggest that, apart from political loyalty (which is perhaps more conditioned by background than by temperament), the tennist is more innovative, more permissive in life-style, less intolerant toward youth and more inclined to view the arts sympathetically than the golfer.

As a few specific indices, I would adduce that the tennist values The New York Times over The Wall Street Journal, and reads The New Yorker at least as conscientiously as U.S. News & World Report; it would be exactly the reverse for the golfer. The tennist also seems less bigoted toward minority groups, even though tennis has had an aristocratic cachet in the past and players were treated like upper servants by the arrogant inheritors of WASP wealth and tennis court dominion.

One form of typology that has gained credence over the years is Sheldon's division of body-builds into the "ectomorphs," "mesomorphs" and "endomorphs," with their corresponding tempermental traits. It seems clear that golf is more a game for the endomorph, who tends toward a heavy build with prominent abodomen and buttocks; while tennis appeals more to the ectomorph, who is leaner, ganglier, and also has a more excitable nervous system.

As much as anything, however, tennists and golfers differ in their humor, which is perhaps the most decisive attribute of personality structure. The tennist often finds the golfer's humor crude and banal; the golfer usually finds the tennist's humor cruel and sardonic. The golfer's humor washes over us, like tepid water; the tennist's humor stings.

Golfers, on the whole, like their own kind of people better than tennists like their own kind of people. Tennists are more critical—of others publicly, and of themselves privately. Golfers are secure in their ignorance; tennists are uneasy in their awareness.

Golfers are also more tolerant, for they demand more tolerance from others. In games-playing, at least, if not in life, they are less compulsive and less competitive personalities. Golf is basically a game of "live and let live" where the duffer can rub along comfortably with the pro; tennis is relentlessly a game of "live or die" where the better player has no compassion for his inferiors. The golfer is ruefully aware of his deficiency, and asks only the kindness not to be reminded of it. But the tennist is the sort of man who keeps reminding him.

In one important respect, golf has all the best of it. The game induces realism, if not humility: if you consistently score 97, you cannot pretend (to others or to yourself) that you score 68, or would if a few breaks had come your way. Each golfer knows exactly where he stands in the firm hierarchy of the game.

Tennis really has no similar touch-stone. Thus, every player fondly imagines that he is at least a niche higher than he is, that under perfect conditions and in "top form" he could take a set from Stan Smith. It is this arrogant inner conviction that makes the tennist so much less palatable a gamesmate than the self-accepting golfer.

Lastly, it must be admitted that in some ways golfers are nicer people than tennists, just as pinochle players are more companionable than devout bridge players. Obviously, this article is written by a fanatical tennist—a man who would never purposely make a bad call against his opponent on the court, but who feels free to be flagrantly unfair to golfers beyond the baseline. For the much-maligned golfer (whatever his other sins) would never take after the tennis player in so unconscionable a fashion.

"*Now* there's *a sore loser…*"

"*Let's go, Fred, the court's open!*"

"We had a happy marriage. Then one day his backhand came unglued and I took a set, then another set, then another..."

Doubles Advice – Attack the Chipmunk

DAVID WILTSE

Down with celebrity tennis tournaments. Any activity that actively encourages a person to make a public spectacle of himself should be banned. We are all human. The perfect fool lies only millimeters beneath the skin in all of us. Some things bring the fool to the top like a surfacing porpoise, and I say down with them.

Most celebrity tournaments allow local citizens to play with the celebrities for a fee. The money is a donation to the charity being benefited. (The charity is the cloak of respectability for the whole affair, but no one is deceived.) Now certainly only a hopeless lover of celebrities would watch such a tournament and only a vain, foolish, celebrity-fawner would play in one. Let me tell you about the one I played in recently.

I was dragooned into entering it when I was grousing that it was taking up all the courts at the resort where I was vacationing. The woman in the lobby selling tickets seemed to take it for granted that I would win—if only I could come up with the $50 entry fee. Now, that puts a lot of pressure on a man, being picked as the odds-on-favorite by the woman in the lobby, especially if she's never seen him play. My wife put more pressure on me: "I don't care what you do. I'm taking the kids to see the covered wagon, anyway."

That's coercion. And then there's the shake-the-hand-that-shook-the-hand syndrome. If I rubbed elbows with Lloyd Bridges and Bruce Jenner, I could dine out for a year, telling lies and entertaining dozens.

As it turned out, I was almost as much of a celebrity as most of the celebrities. It's not all Bill Cosby and Alan King, Ethel Kennedy and Farrah Fawcett on the celebrity circuit, folks. You have to work your way up.

The resort had hired a man in Los Angeles who specializes in such things to deliver a peck of certified stars on the given date. The man promised the top-of-the-line, superstars who outgross their pictures, singers whose name alone means a platinum record.

Well, surprise, surprise. The superstars are busy. The good actors are working. The people who can come to a run-of-the-mill celebrity tournament are the actors who aren't gainfully employed—and usually for good reason.

At our tournament, we set new records for obscurity in public figures. There was the wife of a man who occasionally appears on panel shows. There was a former child star, now 48, who hasn't worked since puberty. There were people who appear in crowd scenes on soap operas. If it's possible to be a celebrity whom absolutely no one has ever heard of—we had him.

Out biggest name was a starlet who sings and acts—it says here—but whose only asset is a body as grotesquely distorted as a cantilevered sundeck. She teetered around the courts gamely, defying the law of gravity, and it must be admitted that she was the only contestant who was always on her toes. She had to be to maintain her balance.

The tournament was a round-robin, the winner being the one with the most total games won. Once I realized Chuck Heston wasn't going to show, I began to get a little steamed. You quickly lose your awe of a person if you have to take his word for it that he's famous. Fearing how I would explain this lunacy once my wife found out the price of the entry fee, I began to play like a man possessed. Not possessed of talent, necessarily, just possessed. When we came to the final round, I was the leader in points! I needed one more game out of the final four to clinch the title!

My partner for the final match was the plucky little singer. I think she got as far as she did by distracting her opponents. It wasn't ability, although she tried hard, because she was absolutely hopeless on low balls —she couldn't see them. Our opponents were a celebrity and a local citizen.

One of our opponents, Ron, was a sprinkler systems contractor, although he could have been a celebrity in his crowd for all anyone knew. He had two very strong points to his game: a long, graceful follow-through and a tremendous-looking warm-up suit. He played his strengths. He never took off the warm-up suit and he followed through gracefully, even when his partner hit the ball. His partner was a man who had appeared on a children's show for nine years—dressed as a chipmunk.

A massed audience of 35 watched with indifference and scorn as we walked onto center court for the final four-game match. My palms were sweaty, my throat was parched, my muscles creaked with tension. It was the largest crowd that had ever looked even approximately in my direction since I walked down the aisle to get my high school diploma. And then I had a funny hat and gown to hide me; now here I was naked from the knees down and expected to perform.

Why was I doing this? Why? Why?

I had entered with the distant hope that I might get to know a celebrity, he might like me and become my friend. At least by distant association, I might warm myself in the media glow. That didn't mean I wanted people actually to watch me play.

The celebrities, on the other hand, suddenly came into their own. They didn't play any better, but they played badly with a lot more verve. Their sportsmanship soared and they applauded each other's shots, smiling away, talking brightly and generally behaving as if it were the first two minutes of Hollywood Squares before the questions start.

The first three games went badly. The chipmunk chattered away, scampering back and forth at the net as if a tomcat was after him. Ron followed through beautifully on every shot, including mine. They used a very sound strategy, hitting every ball at the singer's feet. She swung away, stooping as much as she dared. Somehow, she managed to keep from tipping forward onto her pert little nose. She didn't return any balls, however. I ran back and forth frantically, ravenous to hit a ball, slavering for a poach, an overhead, anything.

It came down to my serve in the final game. Firing cannons and double-faults with equal facility, I stumbled to deuce. The rules called for a sudden-death point. I would serve to the chipmunk, who hadn't returned my bullet yet. All I had to do was put the serve in and I was a winner over 30-odd, and I do mean odd, assembled celebrities. As I put up the ball for my serve, the singer bounced up and down on her toes. First serve over the back fence.

The chipmunk, playing to the dwindling crowd, put his hands to his throat and stuck out his tongue, suggesting I was about to choke. The crowd chuckled. It occurred to me that if a man managed to be seen in 40 million American homes every day for nine years, dressed as a chipmunk or not, he might know something I didn't. I choked as if the Boston Strangler had hold of me, and blooped a cream puff toward the chipmunk.

Screeching as if his tail were caught under a rock, he laced a return off my shoetops. As I bent to half-volley, I noticed Ron following-through on some phantom shot of his own. I missed the real ball, but I hit Ron's back for a winner. Thank God my children weren't there to see me lose to a chipmunk and a warm-up suit.

The Stengler Ploy

WILLIAM
WALDEN

"When should a tennis player run into a net post?" is a question that sooner or later poses itself to thoughtful students of the sport, including me. The answer is not easy to find. Instruction books provide no help. They are full of necessary but dreary how-to's: how to hold the racquet, how to place your feet, how to swing, how to keep score, how to cope with overheads and drop shots and topspins. They also have diagrams showing that if your opponent at A hits the ball to B and runs to C to cut off your return, you should hit the ball to D or E. But if they mention the net post, they do so only fleetingly, in passing. Not a word about its potential strategic importance.

Tennis encyclopedias, from which more should be expected, are no better. They list the winner of the men's singles at Forest Hills in 1962 and of the mixed doubles at Wimbledon in 1924, describe the evolution of the game, give the specifications of the ball and racquet, tell you how to construct a tennis court, suggest what to wear on it, and discuss the advisability of attending tennis camps. They may name the net post among the equipment needed for a tennis court, or quote the rule applying to a ball that hits a net post while in play and bounces into the opponent's court, but that is all. None of the tennis encyclopedias that I own includes "net post" in the index. One contains a Glossary of Lawn Tennis Terms that defines net, net ball, net game, netman, net play, and net stick, but omits net post. In the text, nothing is said either for or against colliding with the net post.

The tennis pros to whom I put the question tended to be evasive. They responded with mumbles, a pained look, a stony stare, an irrelevant comment, an obscenity, and an overemphatic "Never!" Inquiries among fellow players also proved futile—with one exception. A cunning old veteran with whom I had a nodding acquaintance agreed to answer my question, but only if

I promised him the cloak of anonymity. Barry Steng-
ler, as I shall call him, is a short, wiry chap who often
advances to the second or third round of regional
tournaments held for his age group but seldom wins
one (the last tournament he won was restricted to
males over sixty-five years of age and under sixty-five
inches in height). I suspected that he'd be able to
answer me because he knows all the standard tricks
and stalls: shoelace-tying, ball-bouncing before serving, racquet-changing because of a supposedly broken
string, holding up his hand after spotting an impercep-
tible movement among the spectators, grip-wiping,
string-straightening, finger-blowing to dry the sweat,
removal of an imaginary foreign object from his eye,
peremptory ordering of a ball boy from one place to
another, rejecting a ball that a ball boy throws to him,
complaints about where photographers station themselves, protests of linesmen's calls, over-extending the
rest period that follows odd-numbered games, and a
host of other ploys.

I intercepted him at the tennis club late one afternoon when I knew he'd be in an expansive mood—as
he was preparing to leave the court after having won a
ladder match in straight sets from a tall, well-built,
bronzed young man of twenty-three who ran like a
deer and hit picture-book strokes (Barry's strokes are a
living horror). Barry nodded sagely when he heard my
question.

"It's strange that so little attention is paid to the net
post, considering how handsomely it can reward a
player who uses it properly," he told me. "It offers one
of the most effective ways of turning a match completely around."

He paused to retape a racquet grip, then went on:
"The key point to keep in mind about running into a
net post is never to do it accidentally. That's wasted
effort, it's inane. Like a drop shot against a fast player
with good anticipation, it must be saved for special
circumstances and employed sparingly. Certainly no
more than once a match, and probably no more than
once a season. If you're leading handily, there's no
need for it. If you're hopelessly outclassed, it's point-

less, because it can't work miracles. It should be used only during the late stages of an important, tight match.

"Assume you're in the deciding set of such a match. You're serving, it's three-all or four-all, deuce, and there've been no service breaks in this set. Your opponent won the previous set, pulling dead even, and has been coming on strong the last few games. He's been holding his service with comparative ease while you've been struggling with yours. You know he'll do his utmost to break your service now and hold his own through the remainder of the set to win the match. And you also know that he can raise the level of his game the extra notch or two that will beat you. You sense his heightened determination and his steely concentration. Unless his power can somehow be blunted, his upsurge stemmed, he will take this game and with it the match. You have to stop him by creating a distraction—one that will break his rhythm, shatter his concentration, ungroove him, unglue him. This, then, is a perfect time for the net-post gambit."

On the next court, a gangling teenager backpedaled to handle an overhead. Barry watched him smash it into the net. "Ah, the elan of youth," he remarked with a smile. Then he grew serious again. "You have to lure your opponent into giving you an opportunity to run into the net post in a seemingly accidental manner. This isn't difficult. You simply hit a short shot or a drop shot near a sideline, then move in to cut off a down-the-line return. Your opponent, seeing your court open to a crosscourt shot, hits a shallow, sharply angled one.

"You expected this. As he swings, you dash across court to get to the ball, which will probably be out of your reach. You make a heroic effort: you lunge toward it and miss it, but hit what you really intended to hit—the net post."

Barry took time out to restring his racquet, explaining, "You simply cannot trust any living person on the face of this earth to string your racquet to your specifications, no matter how explicit they are. That's why I always string my own racquets." He brooded about this depressing situation for a few moments. "And I do a pretty rotten job of it," he admitted. When he had finished, he played "Swanee River" on the strings to test them, made a wry face, and resumed his narrative. "There are ways *and* ways of running into a net post. If you do it head-on, you can knock yourself out. You'll then probably have to forfeit the match, because when you recover consciousness you'll have a concussion or double vision and be in no shape to continue. On the other hand, if you've prepared for this moment by practicing diligently, you'll achieve a bone-crushing thud that will make the spectators shudder with apprehension, create a maximum of visible damage, and yet inflict a minumum of pain and disability. You'll tear a hole in your shirt and display a large, ugly-looking, blue-black, rapidly swelling bruise on your left forearm or upper arm. If you have executed the maneuver skillfully, you'll also draw blood, which is the most dramatic proof of injury."

Barry swatted the heel of his left sneaker with the face of his racquet several times. Evidently satisfied with the resilience of his heel, he went on. "Notice that I mention the *left* arm. Its only function—unless you hit two-handed backhands or are left-handed—is to toss the ball up for the serve, and even an injured left arm can do that adequately.

"After colliding with the net post you should collapse—fall to the ground in a heap and lie there, out cold, dead to the world, waiting for help from linesmen, the umpire, a doctor, ball boys, your opponent, spectators. They will place you in a chair—a pitiable-looking object, a hollow hulk. You will be fanned, massaged, poured on, given something to drink. But you don't respond immediately. You seem *hors de combat.* The spectators are sympathetic but disappointed at being deprived of the finish of a closely contested, exciting match. Your opponent mutters condolences and confidently expects you to default. The world waits breathlessly for your decision."

Barry picked up a tennis ball and squeezed it several times in his right hand. "Some doctors recommend this for tennis elbow," he confided. "But most players prefer the standard method—hitting balls with a racquet."

"What's your decision?" I asked.

"Not to squeeze them."

"About resuming the match."

"Oh. As you lie there, you and you alone know that the crash, bad as it seemed outwardly, only shook you up a little. You play out the scene, following the script carefully. You come to consciousness slowly. You look dazed. You appear not to recognize the umpire or your opponent. You stand up, wobbly. You shake your head once or twice, as though to clear it. Then you announce faintly, with slurred speech, that you will continue. This is greeted with general disbelief. Voices exclaim, 'No, don't do it!' 'You're not able to!' 'You shouldn't!' And so forth. You wave aside all protests, pick up your racquet, and stumble to the baseline.

"Cheers from the spectators for your courage. ('He's all heart, that fellow!') Your opponent is stunned. The umpire has no choice; he orders the match to resume. Your opponent tries to pick up the pieces and put them together again, but everything is at loose ends. His concentration has been shattered to bits, his rhythm scattered to the winds. He's totally demoralized. He can put up only token resistance. From this point on you should steamroller him without difficulty."

"Has it worked for you?" I asked.

"Every time. But I never used it more than once a season. Sometimes I skipped two or three years. Its theatricality makes it too easily remembered. Besides," he added with a significant look, "there are so many other effective ploys."

"What gave you the notion of using this one?"

"An incident in the 1958 men's singles finals at Forest Hills between Ashley Cooper and Malcolm Anderson. The year before, both players had met in the finals of that same tournament, and Anderson had won in straight sets. In 1958, the match went to five sets, and for most of it Cooper waged an uphill struggle. During an exchange in the hard-fought fifth set, with the score at 6-5, Cooper fell to the ground clutching his right ankle. Writhing with pain, he rose, hopped several times, and fell again. At that point, no one would have given a nickel for his chances. But after a delay, he went on playing, and no more than five minutes later, he walked off the court the victor, having taken the fifth set 8-6.

"I thought over that episode very carefully, and filed it away for future reference. Since then I have used several variations of it."

"What sort?" I asked.

He gathered up his racquets, towel, and other paraphernalia. "Do you really expect me to blabber away my hard-earned bag of tricks?" he asked with a grin. And he departed in the direction of the showers.

"Good!"

"But, honey, you should have asked him if he played tennis before
you built your half!"

"This guy's got it all . . . hand-eye coordination . . . , wonderful footwork and a great repertoire of obscene gestures."

"Hey, Mike, forget we had a game today?"

Sleepwalking with Rod Laver

GORDON FORBES

I have, on occasions, done very odd things in the the night. Most people, I suppose, have dreams, and a few even go for the odd stroll, usually quite harmless and uneventful. My activities are far more complex, and are almost limitless in range and variety. I first became aware of this affliction while at boarding school, when having gone to sleep in my dormitory, as usual, I awoke sitting at my desk doing math. Our classrooms were a separate block of buildings, at least three hundred meters from the dormitory and linked by an unlighted gravel pathway. Perhaps the shock of that excursion and the subsequent cold, dark return to my bed triggered off a chain of strange events which have persisted at erratic intervals throughout my life. On another occasion at school, I awoke in the act of practising place kicks in the dark, empty rugby field. Lesser events were commonplace. I might leap up suddenly and close all the windows, imagining a thunderstorm, actually *hearing* and *seeing* the lightning. Or stand on top of my locker, to avoid a sudden flood, or shout commands or warnings, or dive under my bed to escape avalanches. The bouts come and go—usually triggered off by tense activity during the day. For weeks I may sleep like a child, then suddenly be set upon by nights of hectic activity.

Tense tennis tournaments or Davis Cup matches are, of course, ideal breeding grounds for nightmares.

The United States men's doubles championship took place in Boston in those days, during the week preceding Forest Hills. The doubles combination which Cliff Drysdale and I had drummed up made the event far more interesting and I arrived at the tournament filled with enthusiasm.

"You'll be staying," they told me on arrival, "with

the Furcolos. Rod Laver will also be there and you will be sharing the guest suite."

I was excited. Foster Furcolo was the ex-governor of Massachusetts and lived with his family in a superb old house not far from the club. Besides, Rod, tremendously famous always, was at that time at the height of his fame, as he was about to compete at Forest Hills for the last leg of his Grand Slam. We were firm friends by then, and I knew we would have an interesting time. My faithful friend, Clifford Drysdale, was consulted and relegated to more modest digs, while I made ready to move into the luxury and culture of Bostonian society.

The house was beautiful. It had a hall with a wide and elegant stairway which divided into two on the landing, before giving way to the suites above. On the wall above this landing hung a great sail-fish, a trophy, I think from some heraldic deep sea fishing trip of days past. After climbing the section of stairway beneath the sail-fish, one reached the upper floor and turned immediately left into the suite which Rod and I were to occupy. This elaborate description all seems irrelevant now, just as then it did to me. Only later, after that night, had I cause to examine the topography of the place more carefully.

Rod had already arrived. He was sitting in the bedroom upon one of the beds, surrounded by piles of new tennis equipment. Most of the better players of the circuit were well provided with tennis gear, but I never got used to the quantities and varieties showered upon Laver. He looked up as I entered, with typical Laver-like casualness.

"Hello bastard," he said, although I hadn't seen him since Hamburg. "Look at all this bloody gear. Enough gear here to start a store. And that's only half of it. There's no way I'll ever be able to wear all this lot, unless I change my bloody shirt after every game!"

I felt happy and at home with Rod—he had a mild manner with a sense of humor which often played on understatement. He'd understate almost everything, especially his remarkable successes and superb tennis

ability; like the unbelievable, impossible shots he sometimes pulled out of a hat when they were least expected
and badly needed. These he would scrutinize soberly,
before remarking:

"Not a bad little bit of an old nudge, would you
say?" or: "Rare bit of old arse, that one, don't you
think?"

When Governor Furcolo gave us a Cadillac for the
week, Rod gave it an appreciative look. "Thanks Governor," he said, "now we've got transport!"

Now, sitting on his bed, busy lacing up a tennis
shoe, he waved a hand at the extravagant surroundings
and said. "Choose a bed. It's not much, but it's home!"

There was only one other bed apart from the one
upon which he was sitting, so I established myself upon
it and began unpacking. Rodney told me that he and
Fred Stolle were top seeds for the tournament, and
that Cliff and I would meet them in the quarters.

"Who do we play on the way to the quarters?" I
asked him warily. He had a bad habit of judging other
people's abilities on the strength of his own, thus carv-
ing away the mere possibility of losing before the quarters, at least.

"Oh, teams," he said vaguely. "Dell and Bond.
Hoogs and McManus. Eugene Scott and somebody.
People like that. Just got to keep the ball in play and
give the loose ones a bit of a nudge."

"I see," I said. "You mean just coast through the
early rounds."

He nodded, not even recognising my slight sar-
casm. Competitve tennis, I realized, was a very simple
matter for Rodney George.

I began unpacking and as I did so, an uneasy
thought struck me. Rodney was, as far as I knew,
unaware of my erratic nocturnal behaviour. It was true
that Abe Segal had frequently raved about, "Forbsey
belonging in a strait-jacket at night," or other such
remarks, in various lounges and dressing rooms, but it
was equally true that Abie himself was considered
highly unreliable as a source of factual information
and, in fact, an imminently eligible strait-jacket case
himself—moreover, not only at night.

I conducted a quick consultation with myself about the wisdom of even broaching the subject with Rodney. I'd hardly done anything unusual for weeks, discounting the odd outburst or two and the fact that Cliff informed me one morning that I had pulled him out of bed the previous night and coldly instructed him to get on with the match, as play had to be continuous—an accusation which I felt to be groundless, as I usually had some vague memory of my more positive actions, whereas, on this occasion, I'd had none. Still, Laver was Laver, and I baulked at the idea of taking him completely by surprise, so I decided to mention the thing very casually.

"In case you hear me moving about the room in the dark," I said, idly examining one of the racquet grips at which he continually scraped and whittled, "don't worry. Just put on the light." He looked at me thoughtfully.

"What might you be doing?" he asked.

"I, er, sometimes, very occasionally, well, you know, I, er—."

"Start a revolution," he interrupted. "Don't tell me big Abie wasn't just raving on?"

"Abie exaggerates enormously," I said. "At worst I usually walk quietly round my bed, or give one or two instructions."

He said no more, besides giving me a penetrating look and muttering, "My bloody oath," under his breath once or twice, in a very Australian way.

The Furcolos were a great family, epitomising the warm, but casual hospitality, the lack of pompousness, yet the proper dignity of the true American. We had dinner and a game or two of table tennis before turning in. It was as well that I had warned Rodney. Sometime during that first night, in the light of the moon which poured in through the window, I saw a thin, smallish and vicious-looking animal leap onto my bed and run up the covers towards my face at an alarming rate. Laver or no Laver, action had to be taken. In the nick of time I leapt up, rolled the creature up in the bed covers and, kneeling on my bed, I was busy squeezing the rolled bed cover violently in order to throttle the creature, when Rodney awoke. He sat up immediately.

"What's happening?" he asked, not unreasonable.

"I've got the little devil in here," I cried.

"Who is he?" asked Rodney.

"A thin little bastard," I replied.

Suddenly I threw the rolled up cover on Rodney's bed.

"Have a look if he's dead yet," I commanded.

Rodney backed away. "You have a look," he said.

I began to realize then that something passing strange was going on, but was still in the grip of the dream. Gingerly I unrolled the cover and by the time it was open, I had fully awoken.

"I warned you that I sometimes did things in the night," I said sheepishly. "You should have switched the light on."

"Sorry about that," said Rodney, typically. "Came as a bit of a shock though. Didn't know what you had rolled up in there. Wasn't sure whether you'd managed to kill it. Thought it might jump out. For a moment there I really thought you had something!"

"So did I," I said fervently and quietly thanked my stars that the incident was over and that it had not been worse. Also, to my great relief, I began sleeping like a log, so that it seemed that my night-time performance had been a flash-in-the-pan.

I practiced each morning with Rodney—rigidly effective Harry Hopman type practice which forced you to make every shot with a purpose in mind—not the comfortable, free swinging hit-ups which were so tempting and which made you imagine that you were beautifully in form, and playing like a sort of improved version of Donald Budge.

Ten minutes of forehand crosscourts—ten of forehand to backhand, up the line, ten of backhand to forehand, ten of crosscourt backhands; then all four repeated twice over with alternate players volleying. All that added up to two hours, leaving thirty minutes for practising overheads, services or any special weaknesses. A half-hour practice set completed the three hour session which Rodney insisted we follow. By the end of the week I had never played better, and often in retrospect, I have thought of those far off sessions and said to myself wistfully, "If only! Forbes, if only!"

Cliff and I continued our efficient combination, edging out the American teams by the odd service break—all that is needed in grass court doubles. In the quarters we found ourselves faced by Laver and Stolle, having beaten Donald Dell and Billy Bond in the sixteens. It was strange that, having begun my doubles link-up with Cliff in a state of some uncertainty, we now found ourselves in the quarters of the United States National Doubles, actually discussing positively the possibility of beating the first seeded team.

The evening before the encounter, the four of us drank a few beers together in a mood of good-natured banter. Fred Stolle warned Cliff against hitting, "Those arsey shots off that crappy double hander," and Cliff in turn said that Fred should, "Watch his tramline and not serve too many doubles."

This remark carried a slight edge to it, as Fred never pandered to caution on his second ball, serving it virtually as hard as his first. This resulted in a restless time for the receiver, but also, on Fred's off days, a good many double faults. Rodney said very little except that he thought the four of us should be able to, "Move the ball about a bit out there on fast grass!"

Rodney and I turned in early that night. And I remember clearly that the thought of any unforeseen activity did not even enter my head. I was tired and fell asleep almost at once. Our room was so arranged that the wall which backed up against the stairwell consisted of a long built-in cupboard which Rod and I shared. As Rodney had chosen the bed farthest from the cupboard, my bed was adjacent to it, at a distance of perhaps ten to twelve feet.

Some time late that night, I opened my eyes to find the room full of moonlight. Standing in the cupboard, quite still, was a man whom I could see clearly through the open door. My heart froze as my mind raced through the possible reasons for his presence, finally fastening onto the obvious one. He was there to "get"

Rodney. There was no doubt about it. Rodney was a celebrity and this man, hiding in our cupboard, was an American psychopath, out to do him in. But my bed was between him and Rodney and the thought that he may not be sure which was Rod and which was me, made the situation even more desperate. The headline, "Laver saved when Assassin strikes Thin South African," flashed through my mind. Action had to be taken at once.

Suddenly a daring and subtle plan occurred to me. The cupboard had heavy doors with keys which turned easily. All I had to do, I decided, was to brace myself, leap up, slam the door and lock him in. There was no time to lose so, tensing myself for the deed, I began the countdown. In a state of nervous tension, one moves like lightning. I counted to three, hurled aside the bed clothes, gave a mighty leap, landed besides the cupboard, closed the door with a slam, and turned the key. As the noise died away, I heard an answering rumbling from somewhere in the house, then silence. I leaned for a moment against the cupboard door, weak with relief and overwhelmed suddenly by tiredness. Such was the depth of the nightmare that I was still tightly in its grip. It was then that I noticed Rodney, standing bolt-upright on the far side of his bed.

"Bit of a hell of a bang," he said shakily. "What's happening?"

"There was a guy in the cupboard," I replied, "who was going to get you. I locked him in."

"Oh, really?" said Rodney.

"We'll get him out in the morning," I said.

I was desperately tired and climbed back into bed. The incident was closed, my mind was blank, yet at that moment as I lay back and closed my eyes, the first nudges of reality occurred.

"It's not possible," I remember thinking to myself. "I *couldn't* have actually done *that*. Not again. Not tonight, of all nights!"

But then there was a knocking sound and I opened my eyes. Rodney was standing next to the cupboard, tapping on the door with his knuckles and holding an ear to it.

"Anyone in there?" he said in an urgent whisper. "Who in the hell are you?"

"It's OK, Rodney." I said loudly and he jumped about three inches off the floor, "there's no one in there."

"You just told me there was," he said. "Could have believed you too."

"It's one of my dreams," I said. "I'm terribly sorry. You should have put the light on."

"No time for that," he said. "Just a bloody great bang. A man doesn't think about switching lights on when he thinks he's in a raid. Anyway, I'm opening this cupboard, just to make sure!"

We both watched in silence as he gingerly unlocked the door and opened it. Immediately inside it hung my raincoat on a hanger. Rodney gave it a contemptuous punch.

"Fooled you, you bastard," he said to the coat. "Thought you were going to get us, hey? Hadn't counted on my friend here, had you?"

Now, thirteen years later, the unreality of that particular situation still occasionally strikes me—Rodney Laver, chatting to a raincoat in the middle of a far-off night in Boston!

We slept, eventually. So badly did I want to disassociate myself from the incident that, when I awoke, I found myself still with the faint hope that the whole thing might yet prove to be a dream within a dream.

"I dreamt I had a dream last night," I said to Rod when he finally awoke.

"Your dream couldn't have been as bad as *my* dream," he said with deep conviction.

"Bad, hey?" I asked.

"Nearly crapped myself," he said cryptically. "Going to pay a lot more attention to what Abe Segal says from now on. Now I realize why he sometimes behaves as though he's got someone after him! Always looking over his shoulder, these days, is big Abie. Now I'm beginning to understand why!"

We went down to breakfast after I had made Rodney promise not to tell of the incident. Governor Furcolo looked up as we entered.

"Morning," he said cheerfully. "Quite a night wasn't it?"

I was speechless, but Rodney found words.

"Something happen in the night?" he enquired carefully.

"God-darned sail-fish," said the Governor.

"Sail-fish?" Rodney looked puzzled.

"Been hanging on that wall for nearly eight years now and last night—down he came. Made a mighty bang, too. We kinda thought you might have heard it."

"You hear a bang in the night, Gordon?" he said.

"Can't say I did," I muttered.

"Broke a piece off his tail," said the Governor. "I'll have to get it glued up."

My private theory was that the banging of the heavy cupboard door had dislodged the sail-fish, but it could never be proven. I consoled myself with the thought that there was just a chance that by some remarkable coincidence, the fish had chosen that particular moment to drop from the wall. Just a very small chance. But we never found out.

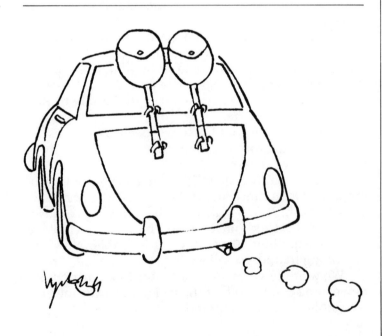